Traditional
BRITISH
COOKING

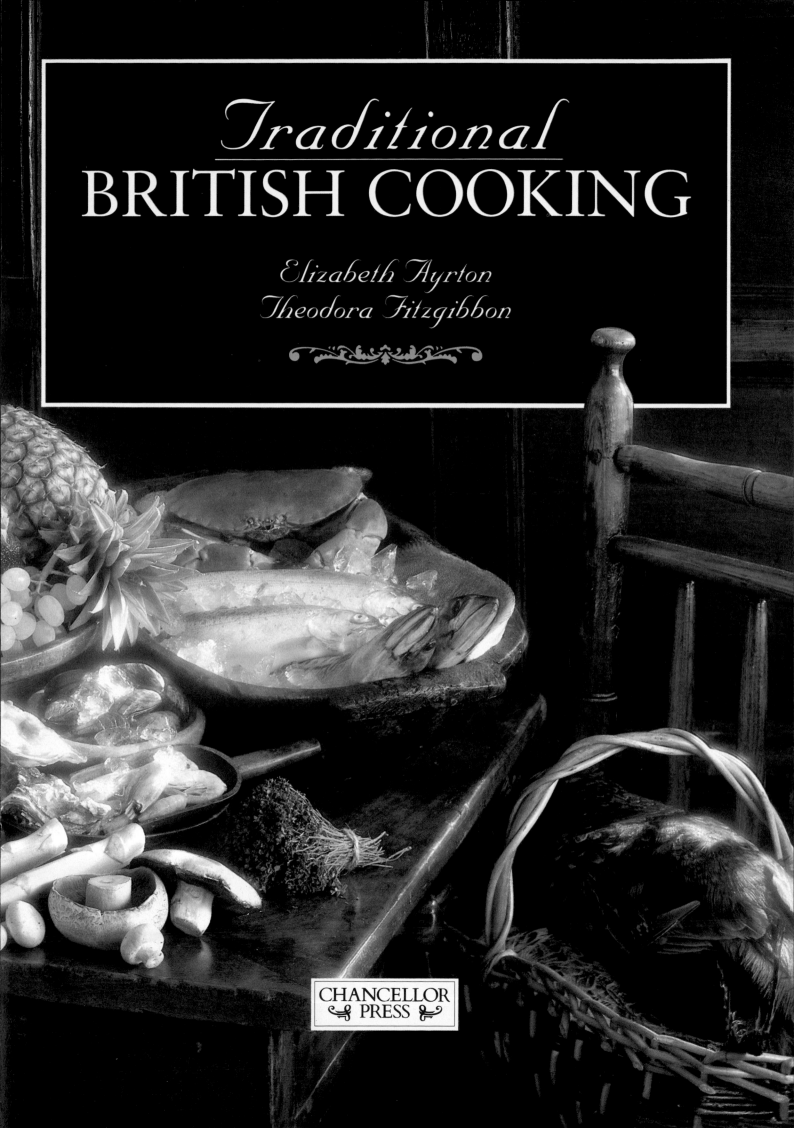

Traditional
BRITISH COOKING

Elizabeth Ayrton
Theodora Fitzgibbon

CHANCELLOR
PRESS

First published in Great Britain in 1985

This edition published in 1993 by Chancellor Press, an imprint of
Reed Consumer Books Limited, Michelin House, 81 Fulham Road,
London SW3 6RB, and Auckland, Melbourne, Singapore and Toronto

ISBN 1 85152 352 9   Printed in China

CONTENTS

INTRODUCTION

On a world map, the United Kingdom looks very small. Yet the cookery within the kingdom varies greatly from region to region, reflecting the history, industry and the fertility of the area. Of course, mass-produced and frozen foods have tended to level out these differences but they are still quite apparent, even today.

A country's history largely determines its cookery traditions and this can be clearly seen throughout the different regions of Britain. Many cultures have left their mark, influencing the eating habits of the inhabitants and bringing new ideas and ingredients to add to their repertoire. Sometimes, when travelling around, the change between one county and another is still very marked not only as regards scenery but also in the idiosyncratic tastes of the residents.

The Saxons were good farmers and used a wide variety of herbs which still dominate many regions – Kentish food, for instance. Many of our old festive dishes are Saxon in origin, such as the wassail bowls with the roasted apples sometimes floating on top or the boar's head with an apple in the mouth. Much of our superb smoked food can be traced to the Danes who knew how to preserve food and smoke fish for long sea voyages. This is particularly noticeable on the Northumberland coast where, even today, the best kippers in Britain are still produced.

The Romans lived in Britain for about three hundred years and everywhere they went they improved methods of growing corn and working the mines. From a culinary point of view perhaps their greatest contribution was to build the wonderful roads, which meant that produce could be transported from one place to another more easily and communications between regions were improved. The Romans loved the East Anglian oysters and other sea food, and, in turn, they introduced Britain to the sweet, succulent cherry.

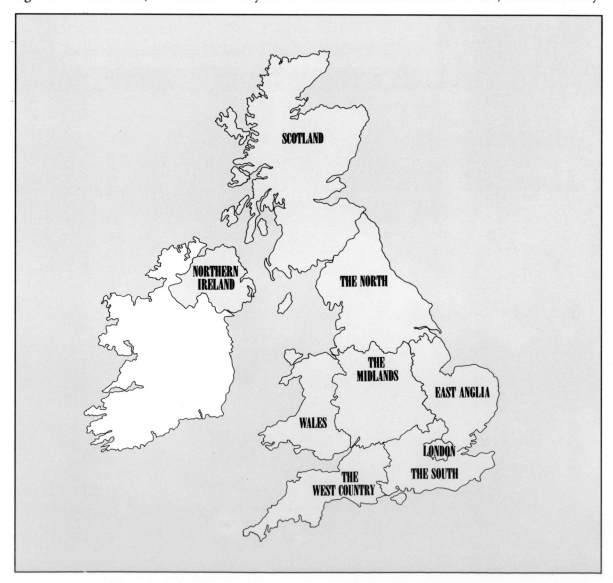

Left:
Conway Castle,
Wales
Below:
Cushendall Bay,
Co Antrim

The Normans brought many new ideas to Britain relating to food and wine. Indeed, many of the names of our most common foods come from Norman French – such as mutton (*mouton*) and beef (*boeuf*).

Since the Middle Ages, London has always offered a greater variety of foods in the markets, and dishes made from these foods, than any other town in Britain. In the twelfth century, a visitor to London, William Fitzstephen, wrote:

'Moreover there is in London upon the river's bank ... a public cookshop. There daily, according to the season, you may find viands, dishes roast, fried and boiled, fish great and small, the corser flesh for the poor, the more delicate for the rich, such as venison and birds both big and little ... Those who desire to fare delicately need not search to find sturgeon or "Guineas-fowl" or "Ionian Francolin", since all the dainties that are found there are set forth before their eyes. Now this is a public cookshop, appropriate to a city and pertaining to the art of civic life.'

Fitzstephen was certainly lucky, for many other travellers refer to the 'rotten meat' and 'rancid oil' to be found in cookshops. In the royal palaces, however, and the town houses of the nobility, the cooking was clearly superlative.

Outside London British cookery seems to divide naturally into nine regions, including Scotland, Northern Ireland and Wales. These last three relate closely to each other because their people are all of Celtic origin and are remote from the great cities and the most prosperous agricultural areas of England. Also, over the centuries all three regions have tried to keep their own culture and traditions alive and separate from those of England.

All three regions have a tradition of good hot meals, well-seasoned and substantial, which a man who has worked hard all day on the land or the sea or, in some cases, down the mines, will be thankful to get inside him before he takes his leisure. Northern Irish dishes are often filled out with their great staple ingredients: potatoes. Scottish and Welsh dishes often take the form of meat or fish stew, sometimes made into a pie.

The dishes of the home counties and the south were of equal excellence. Kent, county of hop-picking and cherry growing, often called 'the Garden of England', has produced a special cuisine in which many dishes, both sweet and savoury, include cherries and sometimes apples and the fine

Kentish cob nuts which, many years ago, were cultivated in special 'nut gardens'.

The Midlands' countryside comprised rich farming land but in the early nineteenth century the growth of industry led to many large industrial conurbations which affected the way their cooking developed. Cities such as Birmingham and Sheffield supported ill-paid factory workers who had to eat as they could, but they also produced and supported the new middle class who wanted satisfying dishes with plenty of meat. Those who came to the 'shires' for hunting also wanted substantial meals after a hard day riding to hounds, and so typical dishes of this region are fine meat pies, good English cheeses, braised meats, and stews enriched with ale or red wine.

At the sheep-shearing festival in the Cotswolds, the traditional foods were great hams as well as pies and many puddings and cold sweets.

In the North, the tradition of the beloved 'high tea' still persists. This was served when men came home from the factory or indoors from the farm and was eagerly awaited by children home from school. A hot meat or fish dish was generally expected as well as potted meat or potted shrimps, brawn or galantine, ham and a variety of scones and cakes. The Singing Hinnies, the Sally Lunn teacake and the Parkin of Yorkshire are all still made today.

The British have always been great travellers and anything liked when abroad has always been tried out when home once more. Admittedly, many of the dishes do not taste the same as in their country of origin, but that is because they have been adapted to suit the taste, climate and ingredients available in this country. The British curry, for instance, is a far cry from the one which originated in India, but it is nevertheless very popular. And throughout British history, other cultures have been welcomed and absorbed, which has added to the richness of the country's heritage.

The traditional food of a country survives because it is the best food which has been tried and tested over a great many years. Such food suits the climate, and the working conditions and uses the best products. Fashion may change tastes in food sometimes almost as fast as it changes the way we dress, but, in the long term, traditional dishes are preferred and remain the favourites.

It is important to know what your own country's food should taste like, because before you have really tasted it, you cannot begin to compare it with other foods from other countries. Britain is fortunate in possessing superb raw materials which, when treated with love and care, produce great dishes which will always be remembered.

In this book we have set down about 20 recipes from each region in the United Kingdom to give a flavour of the individual local ingredients and dishes. As these are traditional recipes, some of them dating back several hundreds of years, butter and cream are freely used, but in all the cakes and pudding recipes margarine can be substituted and a good vegetable oil can be used for frying or roasting.

Elisabeth Ayrton
Theodora Fitzgibbon

Above: Oast houses, Chiddingstone, Kent
Opposite:
Hebden Bridge, Yorkshire

SCOTLAND

Scottish cookery has always differed from that of England south of the border. The commanders of the Roman legions which guarded Hadrian's Wall, which runs from Carlisle to Newcastle, taught the English some of their sophisticated Roman methods of cooking, but they never made friends with the Picts and Scots north of the border and so Scottish cuisine, unlike that of the English, developed late and slowly. From very primitive cooking methods Scottish cuisine developed into the elaborate dishes learnt from English lords who had Scottish estates and from the French who served Mary, Queen of Scots.

Queen Victoria and Prince Albert, when they acquired Balmoral in the nineteenth century, brought with them the elaborate food of the English court. At the same time, they took an interest in offering Scottish dishes to distinguished visitors.

Scottish cooks have always been famous for their excellent baking. Every kind of scone, plain and fancy breads, rich cakes, plain 'keeping' cakes, drop scones and shortbreads were made in manors and castles and the houses of well-to-do merchants in the Scottish cities and ports. Many of these recipes have become world-famous.

There are a number of fine dishes using other ingredients, special roasts of venison and game, stews, soups and 'collops', for example, which are not so well known, and yet are equally satisfying.

Scottish fish, from the lochs, the sea and the fast-running streams and rivers, is superb and the Scots have been, and remain, masters of smoking fish. Their smoked salmon, haddock, kippers and bloaters are unsurpassed.

Heather honey and malt whisky are very much prized and lend their joint flavour to the famous Atholl Brose, which can be made into a drink or turned into a thickened cold sweet like the English Syllabub.

Whisky appears in many Scots dishes. A tablespoon or so improves soups, stews and sauces and gives them a distinctive flavour, quite different from French or English soups which use brandy or reduced red wine.

Aerial view of Eilean Donan Castle, Scotland

POACHER'S POT

Poacher's Pot was originally exactly that – an iron potful of game and venison poached from the nearby woods at great risk to the poacher. Later, the name was used for any rich stew combining game birds and meat and vegetables. This particular recipe comes from Inverness. A preserving pan is generally needed to cook these quantities.

Serves 10–12

1 rabbit or 1.25 kg (2¾ lb) chicken, jointed
2 pigeons, halved
2 old grouse or pheasants or 1 of each, jointed
50 g (2 oz) flour
2 medium turnips, peeled and cut in 2.5 cm (1 inch) cubes
2 large onions, peeled and sliced
3 large carrots, scraped and cut in rings
1 kg (2 lb) cut of venison or 1 kg (2 lb) gammon joint
4 sprigs thyme
4 sprigs sage
4 sprigs parsley
15 g (½ oz) salt
1 teaspoon freshly ground black pepper
1 large Savoy cabbage, outer leaves and hard stalk removed, quartered
300 ml (½ pint) red wine

Preparation time: 1 hour
Cooking time: 2½ hours

1. Place the rabbit and game joints in a bowl, and rub over with flour.
2. Put all the vegetables, except the cabbage, in a very large pot or preserving pan and place the game and rabbit joints on top of them. Put the venison or gammon on top again, in one piece.
3. Add the herbs, salt (if gammon is used, reduce the salt to ¼ oz) and black pepper. Add just enough water to cover all the meat.
4. Cover closely with a double layer of foil, bring to the boil, and then simmer very slowly for 2½ hours. Stir from time to time, in case the vegetables stick to the bottom of the pan.
5. After 2 hours, add the cabbage and the red wine. Make sure at this point that the stock is gently boiling and taste for seasoning.
6. After another half hour lift out the venison or gammon, and carve it into thick slices. Cut the slices in half and put these back into the stew to warm through.
7. To serve, carefully ladle some stew into large soup plates or bowls standing on meat plates, making sure that each one has a large portion of cabbage, a joint or two of the game and some meat, as well as some root vegetables and plenty of gravy. Serve with crusty home-made bread or scones, to mop up the gravy.

LADY TILLYPRONIE'S SCOTCH BROTH

This excellent version of Scotch broth is from Lady Tillypronie's kitchen book, written about 1880.

Serves 6

1 kg (2 lb) breast of lamb or scrag end of neck
5 medium onions, peeled and finely sliced
5 turnips, peeled and finely sliced
3 large carrots, scraped and finely sliced
1.7 litres (3 pints) water
salt
12 peppercorns
1 leek, washed and finely sliced
2 sticks of celery, strings removed, finely sliced
3 tablespoons pearl barley

Preparation time: 20 minutes, plus cooling
Cooking time: 3¾ hours

1. Put the lamb, 3 onions, 3 turnips and 2 carrots into a large pan with the water and seasoning. Bring to the boil, cover and simmer for 3 hours.
2. Allow to get quite cold and then remove all the fat. Pour off the stock and reserve. Take the meat off the bones, discarding the fat and vegetables.

From the top, clockwise: *Poacher's pot, Asparagus soup, Lady Tillypronie's Scotch broth*

3. Wash out the pan, to remove any traces of fat, then return the stock, together with the remaining onions, turnips and carrot, the leek, celery and pearl barley. Cover and simmer for 40 minutes.

4. Cut the lamb into small pieces, add to the broth and boil for another 5 minutes until the meat has warmed through.

ASPARAGUS SOUP

This is an eighteenth century recipe from a manuscript in the Macadam collection, Edinburgh. The peas or spinach help to give it a clear green colour.

Serves 6
20 asparagus spears
900 ml (1½ pints) chicken stock (cubes will do)
225 g (8 oz) green peas or chopped spinach
1 teaspoon sugar
salt
pepper
25 g (1 oz) butter
25 g (1 oz) plain flour
150 ml (¼ pint) milk
6 tablespoons double cream

Preparation time: 15 minutes
Cooking time: 30 minutes

1. Discard all but the top 6–8 cm (2½–3½ inches) of the asparagus spears as the lower part may make the soup bitter. Cut the remainder into 2.5 cm (1 inch) lengths. Reserve a few 1 cm (½ inch) tips for garnishing and cook these separately for 10 minutes in a little boiling, salted water.

2. Bring the stock to the boil, put in the asparagus, the peas or chopped spinach, the sugar and seasoning and boil till the vegetables are tender.

3. Purée the vegetables and stock in a food processor or push through a sieve.

4. Melt the butter in a saucepan, stir in the flour, and add the asparagus purée. Bring to the boil, stirring in the milk.

5. To serve, stir in the cream, and add a few asparagus tips to each bowl.

BAKED SEA TROUT

This fish is often referred to as salmon trout because the flesh is pink, but it is thought by many people to be more delicately flavoured than salmon. The finest of all are caught in the sea lochs of Scotland.

Serves 4–6
1 sea trout, about 750 g (1¾ lb), cleaned
15 g (½ oz) butter
2 teaspoons plain flour
salt
freshly ground black pepper
1 teaspoon lemon juice
1 sprig each parsley, fennel, marjoram and tarragon
or 1 bouquet garni
To garnish:
½ cucumber, finely sliced
sprigs of fennel and tarragon

Preparation time: 5 minutes
Cooking time: 35 minutes
Oven: 200°C, 400°F, Gas Mark 6

1. Spread out a piece of foil large enough to wrap up the fish well. Butter it well and sprinkle with flour, salt and pepper. Lay the fish in the centre.
2. Rub the inside of the fish with salt and pepper, sprinkle in the lemon juice and add the fresh herbs, if available.
3. Wrap up the fish, making a close parcel that will keep the juices in. Lay on a baking sheet and put in a preheated oven for 30 minutes.
4. Remove from the oven and undo the parcel, allowing the juice to run into the baking sheet. Lift the fish very carefully, supporting it at both ends so that it does not break, on to a hot, ovenproof dish.
5. Strain the juice and pour it over. Put the fish back into the oven for 4 minutes, so that the top of the skin is slightly crisped.
6. Serve with slices of cucumber and sprigs of fresh herbs arranged round it.

ARBROATH SMOKIES

Arbroath smokies are small haddock, lightly smoked. They have a fine flavour and texture and make a very good first course for dinner or a main course for lunch or supper. They can be found in most good fishmongers.

4 Arbroath smokies
150 ml (¼ pint) single cream
freshly ground black pepper
watercress sprigs, to garnish

Preparation time: 3 minutes
Cooking time: 10 minutes

1. Bring enough water to boil in a frying pan just to cover the smokies. Put the fish in and simmer for 5 minutes.
2. Lift out the smokies and drain. Pour off the water from the pan. Return the smokies to the pan and pour the cream over them.
3. Simmer very gently, shaking the pan and turning the smokies over for 5 minutes, or until quite tender.
4. Lift the fish on to a serving dish, and pour the creamy sauce from the pan over them. Sprinkle with black pepper and garnish with watercress.

HERRINGS IN OATMEAL

Herrings are much better coated with oatmeal and were always cooked like this by the fishermen. They were a favourite breakfast of Edward VII when at Balmoral.

Serves 6
6 herrings, filleted
salt
freshly ground black pepper
75–100 g (3–4 oz) coarse oatmeal
100 g (4 oz) butter or melted bacon fat
1 tablespoon chopped parsley
1 lemon, thinly sliced

Preparation time: 5 minutes
Cooking time: 10 minutes

1. Rub the herring fillets with salt and pepper.
2. Sprinkle the oatmeal evenly on a board or plate and press both sides of the herrings well into it. The oatmeal will adhere to the oily surface of the fish.
3. Put the butter or bacon fat into a frying pan and heat until it is just sizzling. Fry the herrings for about 3 minutes on each side, or until they are golden brown and crisp.
4. Lift from the pan on to a hot dish, sprinkle the parsley over the fillets and arrange the lemon slices round the edge. Serve immediately, while hot, as a breakfast or supper dish.

From the bottom, clockwise: *Arbroath smokies, Baked sea trout, Herrings in oatmeal*

PARTRIDGE PUDDING

2 partridges or grouse (old birds) or 2 pigeons
450 g (1 lb) braising steak
2 tablespoons plain flour
½ teaspoon salt
¼ teaspoon black pepper
¼ teaspoon dried thyme
¼ teaspoon dried marjoram (optional)
750 g (1½ lb) suet crust (page 122)
1 large onion, peeled and finely sliced
100 g (4 oz) mushrooms, finely sliced
900 ml (1½ pints) good brown stock (beef stock cubes
will do)

Preparation time: 1 hour
Cooking time: 2½ hours

1. Cut the birds in half through the breast bone, using a sharp, heavy knife (you could ask the butcher to do this). Trim the steak and divide into 4 pieces.

2. Season the flour with salt, black pepper and herbs, and roll the pieces of game and steak in it.

3. Roll out the suet crust to 5 mm (¼ inch) thickness and line a 1.5 litre (2½ pint) pudding basin. Roll out a separate circle for the lid.

4. Put the steak in the lined basin and pack the pieces of game on top. Tuck slices of onion and mushroom into all the spaces and sprinkle the remainder over the top.

5. Pour in the stock to about 1 cm (½ inch) below the top of the bowl. Brush the top edge of the crust with a little milk and put on the lid, pinching the edges well together. Cover with aluminium foil, turning it under the rim of the pudding basin, and put a plate on top.

6. Stand the basin in a large saucepan and pour in boiling water to come halfway up the sides. Simmer gently, keeping the saucepan always just on the boil, for 2½ hours. Add more boiling water from time to time, if the level is becoming very low.

7. To serve, stand the basin on a plate and wrap round with a clean cloth. Cut round and lift off the top crust and set on one side, so that the pieces of meat and game can easily be lifted out and the side and bottom crust can be cut in sections.

POACHED SALMON

A recipe for a large party. It will require a fish kettle which, if you have not got one, can be obtained from most good kitchen shops or any shop which sells catering equipment. This recipe works equally well with a middle cut of salmon.

Serves 10

1 salmon, about 5.5 kg (12 lb)
1.75 litres (3 pints) court bouillon:
1 medium onion
1 carrot, scraped
3 sprigs parsley
3 sprigs thyme
3 sprigs tarragon
1 bay leaf
150 ml (¼ pint) dry white wine
1 teaspoon salt
5 peppercorns
1 tablespoon olive oil
To garnish:
½ cucumber, peeled and thinly sliced

Preparation time: 5 minutes
Cooking time: 1 hour

1. Remove fins from the salmon and reserve.
2. Put 1.75 litres (3 pints) of cold water into a fish kettle and add all the other ingredients except the olive oil. Put in the fins and bring to the boil. Boil for 30 minutes.
3. Remove from the heat and add the olive oil (which helps to keep the skin of the fish from breaking) and carefully lower the salmon into the liquid, which should just cover it.
4. Bring back to the boil and simmer gently for 30 minutes. Test with a skewer to see if the flesh leaves the bone easily. Lift out on to a flat serving dish, garnish with thin slices of cucumber and serve at once with Hollandaise sauce, if liked, if it is to be eaten hot.
5. If the salmon is to be eaten cold, it should be allowed to cool in the bouillon and then lifted and allowed to become quite cold in the refrigerator. Serve chilled, but not icy cold, with Mayonnaise and a cucumber salad.

From the left: Partridge pudding, Poached salmon

CHRISTMAS COLD SPICED BEEF AND HOT SOUP

In the lowlands of Scotland, spiced beef was often prepared in large households as a standby which could be served to unexpected visitors at Christmas or New Year. Skirt of beef was generally used, boned and rolled by the butcher, but topside or silverside, though more expensive, can be used without rolling if more convenient. With these there is, of course, no waste.

Serves 6–8
2.75 kg (6 lb) skirt of beef, boned and rolled, bones and trimmings reserved, or 1.75 kg (4 lb) topside or silverside, with extra beef bones
225 g (8 oz) salt
2 teaspoons black pepper
1 teaspoon ground cloves
1 teaspoon dried thyme
1 teaspoon dried marjoram
1 teaspoon cayenne pepper
1 teaspoon paprika
450 g (1 lb) carrots, scraped and sliced
450 g (1 lb) onions, peeled and quartered
1 head celery, cut in 5 cm (2 inch) lengths
2–3 tablespoons whisky (optional)
To garnish:
225 g (8 oz) gherkins, finely sliced

Preparation time: 45 minutes, plus salting and cooling
Cooking time: 3½ hours

1. Lay the skirt of beef out flat, skin downward, and rub in most of the salt. If using topside or silverside, cut 3 slashes about 1 cm (½ inch) deep into the top and rub in salt in the same way. Leave the meat to stand in the refrigerator overnight.
2. The next day, drain off all the liquid and wipe the meat, removing any surface salt. Mix together all the herbs and spices and rub them into the meat, particularly into the slashes in the topside. Roll the skirt up tightly and tie with string in 3 or 4 places. (Topside needs no tying.)
3. Put the reserved bones and trimmings into a large, heavy pan. Place the beef on top, pour in enough cold water to cover and bring slowly to the boil. Remove the scum, cover the pan and simmer gently for 1½ hours.
4. Remove and discard the bones and trimmings. Add all the vegetables, bring to the boil again and simmer for another 1½ hours.
5. Lift out the meat and put it on a large, flat dish. Put a board or a plate on top of it and weights on top. Allow to cool in the refrigerator for about 1 hour.
6. Measure 600 ml (1 pint) of the stock and boil, uncovered, in a small saucepan until reduced by half. Allow to cool and reserve for garnish.

7. Skim the remaining stock for soup. Strain the vegetables and put them through a sieve or food processor. Stir into the stock and taste for seasoning. Add 2–3 tablespoons of whisky if liked.
8. When the beef is almost cold remove the weights and plate and garnish the meat with finely sliced gherkins. Pour the reduced stock very gently over the beef so that the pattern of the gherkins is not disturbed. If the stock has already begun to jell, melt gently until it will pour. Refrigerate the garnished beef for at least another 2 hours. **A**

A The beef will keep well in the refrigerator for 4 days.

CRANBERRY APPLE TART

Serves 6
225 g (8 oz) cranberries, fresh or frozen
2 tablespoons demerara sugar
1 kg (2 lb) eating apples, peeled, cored and finely sliced
1 tablespoon caster sugar
Sweet pastry:
175 g (6 oz) plain flour
75 g (3 oz) butter
75 g (3 oz) caster sugar
3 egg yolks
3 drops vanilla essence

Preparation time: 35 minutes, plus chilling
Cooking time: 35 minutes
Oven: 190°C, 375°F, Gas Mark 5

1. Prick each cranberry with a skewer and put in a saucepan with the demerara sugar and 1 tablespoon of water. Simmer gently for 10 minutes.
2. Put through a sieve or moulin to make a smooth purée and set aside to cool.
3. Meanwhile, make the pastry. Sift the flour into a large mixing bowl. Make a well in the centre and put in the butter, sugar, egg yolks and vanilla essence. Work them together with a spoon and into the flour until you can knead it. Knead lightly until smooth. Wrap the dough in a cloth and chill in the refrigerator for an hour.
4. Remove the dough from the refrigerator, sprinkle with flour and roll out to ½ cm (¼ inch) thickness, roughly the shape of the flan tin. Fold the pastry lightly in half over the rolling pin and lift carefully into the tin and unfold it. Press lightly into the tin with the fingers. (The dough breaks easily and so must be handled gently.)
5. Arrange the apple slices in overlapping circles on the pastry, sprinkle with the caster sugar and put in a pre-heated oven for 15 minutes.
6. Remove from oven, quickly pour over the cranberry purée and put back into the oven for another 10–15 minutes.

From the top:
*Cranberry apple tart,
Christmas cold spiced
beef and hot soup*

18

SCOTCH COLLOPS

Collops is an old word (Scandinavian in origin) for slices or pieces of meat. In Scotland, a dish of collops is traditionally served on Burns Night, the 25th of January. Venison is sometimes used, but lamb or steak are more easily available and just as good.

Serves 6
75 g (3 oz) butter
225 g (8 oz) mushrooms, sliced
12 lamb leg steaks, about 13 cm (5 inches) by 5 cm (2 inches) by 5 mm ($\frac{1}{4}$ inch); or
1 kg (2 lb) frying steak (flash fry steak is excellent) cut into pieces of the same size as above
25 g (1 oz) plain flour
600 ml (1 pint) good meat stock (beef stock cube will do)
12 small forcemeat balls (see below)
salt
freshly ground black pepper

Preparation time: 25 minutes
Cooking time: 30 minutes

1. Melt the butter in a large frying pan and fry the mushrooms lightly. Transfer them to a large, shallow saucepan.
2. Add the collops of meat to the frying pan. Fry for 4 minutes on each side, then lay them on top of the mushrooms.
3. Stir the flour into the frying pan and add the stock a little at a time, stirring well. Bring just to the boil so that it thickens to the consistency of thin cream.
4. Pour this sauce over the collops and mushrooms, add the forcemeat balls, season, and put the saucepan on a gentle heat. Cover and simmer gently for 10 minutes.
5. Lift the collops and forcemeat balls on to a heated serving dish, pour over the sauce and mushrooms and serve immediately.

HERB FORCEMEAT BALLS

Serves 6
175 g (6 oz) breadcrumbs
50 g (2 oz) shredded suet
50 g (2 oz) bacon, finely chopped and fried crisp
2 teaspoons finely chopped parsley
2 teaspoons dried herbs or 4 teaspoons finely chopped fresh marjoram, thyme and sage
salt
freshly ground black pepper
1 egg, beaten well
40 g (1$\frac{1}{2}$ oz) butter

From the top: Roast venison, Scotch collops with Herb forcemeat balls

Preparation time: 5 minutes
Cooking time: 6 minutes

1. Mix together the breadcrumbs and the suet in a bowl.
2. Add the bacon, parsley, herbs, salt and pepper. Stir the beaten egg into the mixture.
3. Form into little balls about 2.5 cm (1 inch) in diameter. Melt the butter in a frying pan, add the forcemeat balls and fry for 6 minutes.

ROAST VENISON

Marinading for 24 hours, as in this traditional Scottish recipe, brings out the delicious flavour and prevents the meat from being dry.

Serves 6
1.5–2 kg (3$\frac{1}{2}$–4$\frac{1}{2}$ lb) piece of venison, saddle or haunch
175 g (6 oz) softened butter
25 g (1 oz) plain flour
Marinade:
300 ml ($\frac{1}{2}$ pint) red wine
1 carrot, scraped and sliced
1 medium onion, peeled and sliced
1 sprig thyme
1 bay leaf
1 teaspoon peppercorns
2 tablespoons wine vinegar
2 tablespoons olive oil
1 garlic clove
2 teaspoons soft brown sugar

Preparation time: 20 minutes, plus cooling and marinading
Cooking time: 2–2$\frac{1}{2}$ hours
Oven: 180°C, 350°F, Gas Mark 4

1. The day before you intend to serve the venison, boil all the marinade ingredients together for 20 minutes. Allow to cool.
2. Place the venison in a large china or glass bowl, pour over the marinade and stand in a cool place for 24 hours. Turn the joint and spoon the marinade over it from time to time.
3. When ready to cook the venison, remove it from the marinade and drain. Spread it with the softened butter, lay in a roasting dish and roast in a preheated moderate oven for 2–2$\frac{1}{2}$ hours. Baste twice during the cooking time.
4. Remove the venison from the roasting tin and keep warm on a serving dish. Pour off any surplus fat from the tin and stir the flour into the pan juices over a gentle heat. Strain the marinade liquor and add it very gradually to the roasting tin, beating with a wire whisk until smooth. Taste for seasoning and then simmer for 5 minutes. Serve separately.

KEDGEREE

Kedgeree is a version of an Indian dish –
Khichri – and was first brought back by
members of the East India Company. It was a
famous breakfast or supper dish in Scotland in
the eighteenth and nineteenth centuries.

*275 g (10 oz) long-grain rice, cooked so that each
grain is dry and separate*
*175 g (6 oz) cooked smoked haddock, bones and skin
removed, finely flaked*
2 eggs, hard-boiled and finely chopped
3 tablespoons butter or soft margarine
salt
freshly ground black pepper
1 tablespoon chopped parsley

Preparation time: 5 minutes
Cooking time, including pre-cooking of
ingredients: 35 minutes

1. Mix the rice, haddock and hard-boiled eggs
lightly together.
2. Melt 2 tablespoons of the butter in a saucepan,
without allowing it to colour. Stir in the rice
mixture and toss until hot through. Add salt and
black pepper.
3. To serve, pile the kedgeree in a flat dish, dot
with remaining butter, sprinkle with parsley and
serve very hot with toast and butter.

SCOTCH EGGS

Serves 6
6 eggs
350 g (12 oz) pork sausagemeat
2 teaspoons finely chopped parsley
¼ teaspoon dried marjoram
¼ teaspoon dried sage
¼ teaspoon dried thyme
½ teaspoon grated lemon rind
salt
coarsely ground black pepper
1 egg, beaten
150 g (5 oz) fine white breadcrumbs
vegetable oil for deep frying

Preparation time: 25 minutes
Cooking time: 10 minutes

1. Hard-boil the eggs and cool under running
water. Shell them carefully and set on one side.
2. Mix the sausagemeat with the herbs, lemon
rind, salt and pepper, working them well in with a
wooden spoon.
3. Divide sausagemeat into 6 pieces and flatten by
rolling each piece on a floured board. Put an egg

on each piece and shape the sausagemeat round to
form an even layer approximately ½ cm (¼ inch)
thick.
4. Roll the covered eggs in the beaten egg and
then the breadcrumbs, pressing them well in.
5. Heat the oil in a deep-fryer to 180°C, 350°F, or
until a cube of bread browns in 30 seconds.
Carefully put in the eggs, 3 at a time, frying them
for 4–5 minutes, turning once, until they are a
deep golden brown. Drain well on kitchen paper.

WHITE DEVIL

This splendid strongly flavoured dish used to be
served at the Café Royal, Edinburgh.

*4 chicken breasts, boned and skinned, about 150 g
(5 oz) each, or 4 fillets of smoked haddock,
skin removed*
15 g (½ oz) butter

salt
freshly ground black pepper
Devil sauce:
$\frac{1}{2}$ teaspoon turmeric
$\frac{1}{2}$ teaspoon cayenne pepper
1 teaspoon dry English mustard
$\frac{1}{4}$ teaspoon salt
$\frac{1}{2}$ teaspoon white pepper
300 ml ($\frac{1}{2}$ pint) double cream
To garnish:
8 × 5 cm (3 × 2 inch) puff pastry triangles,
baked and reheated

Preparation time: 10 minutes
Cooking time: 40 minutes
Oven: 180°C, 350°F, Gas Mark 4
then: 200°C, 400°F, Gas Mark 6

---

1. If using chicken breasts, lay them on a large buttered sheet of foil, sprinkle with a little salt and pepper and fold the foil over to make a closed parcel. Lay on a baking sheet and bake in a preheated moderate oven for 30 minutes. Allow to cool and remove from the foil. If using haddock fillets, poach in boiling, salted water for 10 minutes, then drain. **A**

2. Lightly butter a small, shallow, ovenproof dish and lay the chicken breasts or haddock fillets in it.

3. Mix the turmeric, cayenne pepper, mustard, salt and pepper into the cream and beat just until it begins to thicken.

4. Pour the Devil sauce over the chicken or fish and put into a preheated hot oven for 8–10 minutes, or until it just begins to brown. Do not allow it to boil. Serve with the rough puff pastry triangles arranged round the edge of the dish.

A The chicken or fish may be cooked in advance and kept in the refrigerator. The chicken will keep for 2 or 3 days; the haddock is better prepared on the day it is to be used.

From the left:
*Kedgeree, Scotch eggs,
White devil*

SCOTCH SHORTBREAD

This is a rich shortbread which is very simple to make as it requires no kneading.

Makes an 18 cm (7 inch) round
100 g (4 oz) butter
50 g (2 oz) caster sugar
225 g (8 oz) plain flour
salt
caster sugar, for serving

Preparation time: 10 minutes
Cooking time: 45–60 minutes
Oven: 120°C, 250°F, Gas Mark ½

1. Cream together the butter and sugar, until very soft.
2. Beat in the flour and the salt.
3. Roll out to 2.5 cm (1 inch) thickness and put in a greased 18 cm (7 inch) round flan tin. If it will not roll well, it can be pressed into the tin by hand.
4. Prick it well with a fork and lightly mark into sections.
5. Bake for 45 minutes in a preheated oven until golden brown. If liked, sprinkle with caster sugar before serving.

OATCAKES

Makes 6–8
225 g (8 oz) fine oatmeal, plus a little for sprinkling
¼ teaspoon salt
½ teaspoon bicarbonate of soda
2 teaspoons melted butter or bacon fat
300 ml (½ pint) hot water

Preparation time: 10 minutes
Cooking time: 5 minutes

1. Put the oatmeal into a bowl with the salt and the bicarbonate of soda.
2. Pour in the melted butter and add enough hot water to make a soft paste. Turn on to a board sprinkled with oatmeal and roll out very thin – 3 mm (⅛ inch) thick.
3. Rub with a little more oatmeal, cut into a large round and then cut across into 6 or 8 pieces.
4. Slide the cakes carefully on to a hot griddle (or into a heavy frying pan) and cook over a moderate heat until they begin to curl up. They should not be turned over. Serve hot or cold with butter.

SELKIRK BANNOCKS

Bannocks are round, flat loaves, traditionally cooked on a griddle but now usually baked in the oven. Many Scottish towns had their own recipes and there were special bannocks made for different feast days. The Selkirk bannock appears in the mid-nineteenth century, first made by a baker called Robbie Douglas.

Makes 3 bannocks
450 g (1 lb) strong white flour
1 teaspoon salt
75 g (3 oz) butter
300 ml (½ pint) warm milk
75 g (3 oz) caster sugar
25 g (1 oz) fresh yeast or 15 g (½ oz) dried yeast
275 g (10 oz) sultanas, soaked in hot water for 30 minutes
1 egg, beaten

Preparation time: 30 minutes, plus 1¾ hours rising
Cooking time: 20 minutes
Oven: 200°C, 400°F, Gas Mark 6

1. Mix together the flour and salt in a large mixing bowl and then rub in the butter.
2. Put the milk in a pan over gentle heat and stir in the sugar until it is dissolved.
3. Remove from the heat and stir 2 tablespoons of this milk mixture into the yeast, until it makes a smooth paste. If using dried yeast, pour half the warmed milk (it should only be lukewarm) into a bowl and sprinkle on the yeast. Whisk well and leave until the yeast becomes frothy (about 15 minutes). Add the rest of the milk to the yeast and beat well into the flour.
4. Collect the dough into a ball, place on a floured board and knead for 5 minutes until the dough is smooth and elastic.
5. Shape the dough into a ball, put it into a warmed bowl and cover with a clean damp cloth. Stand the bowl in a warm place (such as the warming drawer) for 30 minutes.
6. Knead the sultanas gently into the dough, making sure they are evenly distributed.
7. Shape the dough into a ball again, cover as before, and stand in a warm place for a further 15 minutes or until it has almost doubled in size.
8. Divide the dough into 3 equal pieces, shape each into a smooth ball and place each on a lightly buttered baking sheet. Cover again with clean damp cloths and put in a warm place to rise for 15 minutes.
9. Flatten the balls down so that they become approximately the size of dinner plates and brush over with beaten egg. Cover again and return to stand in a warm place for a further 45 minutes.
10. Put into a preheated, hot oven and bake for 20 minutes, or until golden brown.

From the left: *Scotch shortbread, Oatcakes, Selkirk bannocks*

DUNDEE CAKE

The famous light but rich fruit cake which will keep for several weeks.

Makes one 23 cm (9 inch) diameter cake
450 g (1 lb) butter
175 g (6 oz) soft brown sugar
6 tablespoons orange juice
4 tablespoons lemon juice
grated rind of 1 orange
grated rind of 1 lemon
5 eggs, beaten
175 g (6 oz) currants
175 g (6 oz) sultanas
100 g (4 oz) raisins, chopped
100 g (4 oz) candied pineapple (optional)
100 g (4 oz) blanched almonds
50 g (2 oz) crystallized ginger, chopped (optional)
75 g (3 oz) cherries, chopped
75 g (3 oz) mixed peel, chopped
450 g (1 lb) self-raising flour
To decorate:
12 whole, blanched almonds
milk

Preparation time: 15 minutes
Cooking time: 2 hours
Oven: 180°C, 350°F, Gas Mark 4
then: 150°C, 300°F, Gas Mark 2

---

1. Line a 23 cm (9 inch) diameter cake tin with greased greaseproof paper to 1 cm ($\frac{1}{2}$ inch) above the top of the tin.
2. In a large mixing bowl, cream together the butter and sugar and add the juices and grated rinds of the orange and lemon. Beat the eggs into the mixture.
3. Mix together all the remaining ingredients and fold into the mixture.
4. Fill the tin not more than two-thirds full and make a deep depression in the centre.
5. Dip the whole, blanched almonds in milk and arrange them on the top of the cake. Put the cake in a preheated oven and bake for 1 hour.
6. Reduce the oven temperature and bake for another 1 hour. Cover the top with a piece of foil if it is browning too much.
7. Test with a fine skewer pushed into the centre of the cake: if the skewer comes out clean, the cake is done. Place the tin on a wire tray to cool, then turn out and cool completely on a wire tray.

BLACK BUN

Famous throughout Scotland since the eighteenth century, Black Bun was often made at Christmas, when it was sometimes called Yule Cake. The filling is much like a rich, black Christmas pudding, but the delicate envelope of pastry gives it a special character. It requires neither eggs nor sugar.

Serves 10–12
Pastry:
450 g (1 lb) plain flour
$\frac{1}{4}$ teaspoon salt
225 g (8 oz) butter
Filling:
350 g (12 oz) self-raising flour
1 teaspoon cinnamon
$\frac{1}{4}$ teaspoon black pepper
$\frac{1}{4}$ teaspoon nutmeg
450 g (1 lb) seedless raisins
450 g (1 lb) currants
50 g (2 oz) mixed peel (optional)
50 g (2 oz) glacé cherries, chopped
100 g (4 oz) blanched almonds, coarsely chopped
2 tablespoons whisky
milk
2 egg yolks, beaten

Preparation time: 30 minutes, plus cooling
Cooking time: 2$\frac{1}{2}$ hours
Oven: 180°C, 350°F, Gas Mark 4

---

1. Mix the flour and salt together and rub in the butter till you have a crumb-like consistency. Mix in 1 tablespoon of very cold water. If the dough is still crumbly, add another and stir and mix until it will come away from the bowl in one piece, leaving the bowl clean.
2. Flour a board and roll the pastry out to a little less than 5 mm ($\frac{1}{4}$ inch) thickness. Grease either a 25 × 13 cm (10 × 5 inch) bread tin, or a loose-bottomed 20 cm (8 inch) cake tin. Line the bread or cake tin, moulding the pastry against the sides and making sure there are no holes. Set aside a piece for the lid.
3. Mix all the dry ingredients for the filling together and then add all the fruit and the almonds. Stir well together. Add the whisky and stir in and then enough milk to bring it to a stiff consistency.
4. Fill the tin and smooth off flat at the top. Roll out the pastry lid and lay it on loosely so that the inside can rise a little. Thrust a long skewer through the lid and filling, right to the bottom, in about 8 places. Lightly prick the lid all over with a fork. Brush over with the beaten egg yolks.
5. Put the tin in a preheated oven and bake for 2$\frac{1}{2}$ hours.
6. Allow the bun to stand in the tin on a wire tray for 30 minutes before turning out.

From the left: *Dundee cake, Black bun*

FLUMMERY

Flummery occurs in manuscript menus for feasts as early as the fifteenth century. The ingredients varied, but the basis was always soaked cereal, the liquid from which sets to a clear jelly. This is flavoured with orange juice or rosewater and topped with cream and honey, with or without alcohol.

Serves 6
4 tablespoons oatmeal, soaked for 48 hours
in 900 ml (1½ pints) cold water
12 tablespoons orange juice
2 tablespoons caster sugar
150 ml (¼ pint) double cream
To decorate:
grated rind of 2 oranges
4 tablespoons clear honey
2 tablespoons whisky or brandy
150 ml (¼ pint) whipped cream

Preparation time: 10 minutes plus soaking and setting
Cooking time: 10 minutes

1. Stir the soaked oatmeal and then strain off the liquid into a saucepan. Discard the oatmeal. Add the orange juice and sugar to the liquid, bring to the boil and boil, stirring continuously, for about 10 minutes, or until the mixture is very thick.
2. Allow to cool until tepid and then stir in the cream.
3. Pour the mixture either into one large flat dish or individual dishes and put in the refrigerator to set. (Allow approximately 1 hour.)
4. When ready to serve, sprinkle with grated orange rind, pour over the honey, then the whisky or brandy and top with whipped cream.

SCOTCH PANCAKES

These pancakes are usually made for high tea and served hot with butter and jam.

Makes 18
350 g (12 oz) self-raising flour
½ teaspoon salt
1 egg, beaten
15 g (½ oz) butter, melted
600 ml (1 pint) milk

Preparation time: 5 minutes
Cooking time: 7–8 minutes

1. Sieve together the flour and the salt.
2. Combine the egg and melted butter. Add slowly to the flour and beat well in.
3. Mix in the milk, beating well, to make a batter

the consistency of thick cream.
4. Heat a well-greased griddle or heavy frying pan, and drop tablespoonfuls of the batter on it, at least 2.5 cm (1 inch) apart.
5. Cook for 3–4 minutes until bubbles appear on the surface, then turn and cook on the other side until brown.

TREACLE PUDDING

Treacle recipes were very popular in Scotland in the eighteenth century.

Serves 6
225 g (8 oz) plain flour
75 g (3 oz) shredded suet
50 g (2 oz) soft brown sugar
$\frac{1}{4}$ teaspoon salt
1 teaspoon bicarbonate of soda
1 egg, beaten
5 tablespoons golden syrup
65 ml (2$\frac{1}{2}$ fl oz) milk
1 teaspoon lemon juice

Preparation time: 15 minutes
Cooking time: 2 hours

1. Mix together the flour, suet, brown sugar, salt and bicarbonate of soda in a large bowl. Beat in the egg, 3 tablespoons of the syrup and the milk and continue to beat until the mixture is a soft consistency.

2. Pour the batter into a greased 1.25 litre (2 pint) pudding basin. There should be about 5 cm (2 inches) between the mixture and the top of the bowl to allow room for the pudding to rise.

3. Cover the basin tightly with a double layer of foil and put a plate or saucer on top. Stand the basin in a large saucepan with enough boiling water to come about halfway up the side of the basin. Boil steadily for 2 hours, topping up with boiling water whenever necessary.

4. Turn out on to a warmed plate and serve with the remaining syrup warmed in a small saucepan and sharpened with lemon juice.

From the left:
Flummery, Scotch pancakes, Treacle pudding

29

The NORTH

Cumbria, Durham, Lancashire, Yorkshire, Northumberland

This vast area of England stretches from Hadrian's Wall in the north to the Yorkshire moors and Forest of Bowland in the south. It covers several counties in all, in which soil, climate and basic ingredients vary considerably. The people's needs used to vary too, for what was required in spacious rural areas was very different to what was needed in built-up industrial zones.

As might be expected, certain dishes have stayed within their boundaries, such as in the mountainous Lake District, where the secret of the delicious Cumberland sausage, sometimes 4 feet long, is still preserved, as well as the rare fish, the char, which lives at the bottom of Lake Windermere. The Cumberland Tatie-Pot differs from the Lancashire Hot Pot and the fine potted shrimps are loyal to Morecambe Bay in Lancashire. There are many local fish dishes traditional to the North East coast.

The bleak, windswept Yorkshire Moors, home of the Brontë family, are famous for the delicate Yorkshire curd cakes which are still sold in the main street of Haworth; the moors too, are rich in game and wild berries. High teas abound with home-baked scones, cakes and potato dishes, as well as many different sorts of pies, both meat and fruit. The eating of food is a hearty tradition built up over the years by a hardy people who have worked hard in all weathers and have eaten well when the day's work was done. They have a mixture of Celtic, Roman, Saxon and Scandinavian ancestry which is apparent in their taste for many different dishes.

Salting and smoking are the oldest methods of preserving food, and were probably brought to England by the Vikings. There are many famous local cures for hams, pork and fish. Indeed, the first York ham is said to have been smoked with the sawdust of oaks used in building York Minster. The finest undyed kippers are still to be found at Craster in Northumberland.

Hebden Bridge, Yorkshire

COCKLE SOUP

Serves 6
40 cockles
2 heaped tablespoons butter
2 heaped tablespoons flour
600 ml (1 pint) creamy milk
2 tablespoons finely chopped onion
2 tablespoons finely chopped celery
2 tablespoons finely chopped parsley
salt
freshly ground black pepper
To garnish:
4 tablespoons single cream

Preparation time: 30 minutes
Cooking time: 30 minutes

1. Scrub the shells of the cockles well under cold running water to get rid of grit and sand. Discard any that are already open.
2. Put them in a large saucepan covered with sea-water, or well-salted water.
3. Bring gently to the boil, shaking the pan from time to time; as soon as the shells open they are ready. Do not continue cooking as this can toughen them. When cooled strain the cockles, reserving the stock. Remove the cockles from the shells with a sharp knife.
4. Strain the stock again and set aside, making it up to 900 ml (1½ pints) if necessary with water.
5. Melt the butter in a saucepan, stir in the flour and let it cook for 1 minute. Add the cockle stock, stirring to avoid lumps, and when smooth add the milk the same way. When it is smooth add the onion and celery and cook for about 5–7 minutes or until soft. Add the parsley and season to taste.
6. Finally add the cockles, heat through and serve in warmed soup bowls with a little cream floating on each bowl.

SOWERBY SOUP

Serves 6–8
25 g (1 oz) butter
750 g (1½ lb) onions, peeled and finely sliced
450 g (1 lb) tomatoes, skinned
2.3 litres (4 pints) boiling water
1 tablespoon medium oatmeal
salt
freshly ground black pepper

Preparation time: 10 minutes
Cooking time: 1 hour

1. Heat the butter in a heavy-bottomed saucepan and cook the onions in it gently, until they have softened but have not browned.

2. Add the tomatoes and cook for a few minutes. Pour over half the boiling water, bring back to the boil then lower the heat and simmer for about 30 minutes.
3. Remove from the heat and blend the soup in a liquidizer.
4. Boil the oatmeal in the remaining water for 10 minutes, then pour in the blended onions and tomatoes.
5. Return to the heat and cook for 20–25 minutes. Season to taste and serve hot.

BAKED LAKE TROUT

4 sprigs fresh parsley, finely chopped
4 sprigs lemon thyme, finely chopped
75 g (3 oz) butter
4 lake trout, weighing about 450 g (1 lb) each,
cleaned and washed
salt
freshly ground white pepper
150 ml (¼ pint) dry white wine
To garnish:
lemon wedges
parsley sprigs

From the left: *Cockle soup, Sowerby soup, Baked lake trout, Potted char*

Preparation time: 15 minutes
Cooking time: 30 minutes
Oven: 180°C, 350°F, Gas Mark 4

1. Mix the chopped herbs into 50 g (2 oz) of the butter. Divide the herb butter into 4 and put a piece into the cavity of each fish.
2. Lay the fish head to tail closely in an ovenproof dish and season to taste. Pour the wine over, cover with foil and bake in the preheated oven for about 20 minutes.
3. Take out and add the remaining butter cut into small pieces, cover again and put back for a further 10 minutes.
4. Serve garnished with lemon wedges and parsley sprigs.

POTTED CHAR

The char is a little known member of the salmon family, which is confined to very deep lakes. It is most common in Windermere in the Lake District, where it is a local delicacy, only caught in the spring. The flesh of the fish is pinkish and the flavour very delicate. Between 1600 and the 1850s, it was considered a fine breakfast dish with toast. Potted char used to be put into extremely fine hand-painted ceramic pots which are now collectors' items.

1 teaspoon vinegar
6 char, cleaned
2 teaspoons lemon juice
100 g (4 oz) butter
pinch of ground mace
3 tablespoons melted butter

Preparation time: 35 minutes
Cooking time: 5 minutes

1. Add the vinegar to the water of a steamer. Place the char in the steamer and steam for about 5 minutes until the fish leaves the bones.
2. Lift out, then skin and flake the fish, removing the bones.
3. Place the fish in a bowl and mash it with the lemon juice, the butter and a pinch of mace to taste. Blend very well.
4. Press into 4 pots. If the char is not to be eaten at once, pour the melted butter over the tops. Let it set firmly.
5. Serve with toast or brown bread and butter.
Variation: Brown trout are also delicious potted.

PICKLED RED CABBAGE

Traditionally this is served with Lancashire hotpot, and also with Cumberland Tatie-pot. It is also very good with cold meats or cheese. Leave to mature for 1–2 months before use.

1 medium-size red cabbage, weighing about 900 g
(2 lb), shredded finely
cooking salt
600 ml (1 pint) white malt vinegar
1 tablespoon sugar
1 tablespoon mixed pickling spice
a few slices raw beetroot, if possible

Preparation time: 30 minutes, plus marinating
Cooking time: 10 minutes

1. Place the shredded cabbage in a large roasting pan, sprinkle with cooking salt, cover and leave to stand overnight.
2. The next day, strain off the salty liquid and pack the cabbage into large wide-necked jars, preferably with screwtops lined with plastic. (Do not use tops which are metal alone as they will corrode.)
3. Boil up the white vinegar with the sugar and pickling spice for about 10 minutes, then allow to cool.
4. Pour the cooled pickling vinegar over the cabbage, making sure it is well covered. If possible add a slice of raw beetroot, peeled, to each jar as this maintains a good, red colour.
5. Cover at once, using greaseproof paper and string if plastic-lined tops are not available.
6. Leave a month if possible. Pickled cabbage will keep for a year, if unopened.

CUMBERLAND TATIE-POT

Serves 4–6
900 g (2 lb) middle neck of lamb, boned and trimmed
(ask the butcher to do this)
350 g (12 oz) black pudding
750 g (1½ lb) potatoes, peeled and thickly sliced
3 large onions, peeled and sliced
salt
freshly ground black pepper
450 ml (¾ pint) hot beef stock
1 tablespoon melted dripping or butter

Preparation time: 30 minutes
Cooking time: 3 hours
Oven: 160°C, 325°F, Gas Mark 3

1. Cut the lamb into convenient serving pieces.
2. Slice the black pudding into pieces about 2.5 cm (1 inch) thick.

3. Using a deep casserole, layer potatoes, onions, lamb and black pudding in that order, seasoning well and finishing with a thick layer of potatoes.
4. Pour over the stock to barely cover, grease the lid slightly and put it on the casserole.
5. Cook in the preheated oven for about 2 hours, then take off the lid and brush the potatoes with melted dripping or butter and sprinkle with salt.
6. Return to the oven without the lid for about 30 minutes until the potatoes are nicely browned.

BOILED PICKLED PORK AND PEASE PUDDING

This is still a very popular dish in Yorkshire and other northern counties. Pease pudding is sold separately in butcher's shops and sometimes served with bacon for breakfast.

Serves 8–10
1.4–1.6 kg (3–3½ lb) pickled pork, shoulder or hand,
soaked for 4 hours
1.7 litres (3 pints) water
2 whole cloves
4 large onions, halved
6 large carrots, halved
4 sticks celery, chopped
4 white turnips, halved
6 black peppercorns
1 sprig fresh parsley
1 sprig fresh thyme
750 g (1½ lb) yellow split peas, soaked overnight
25 g (1 oz) butter
2 egg yolks (optional)
1 teaspoon Worcestershire sauce
salt
freshly ground black pepper

Preparation time: 30 minutes, plus soaking
Cooking time: 3¼ hours

1. Place the pork and the water in a very large saucepan and bring to the boil.
2. Stick the cloves into one of the onion halves, then add to the pan with all the vegetables, the peppercorns and herbs. Simmer the meat and vegetables for about 1½ hours.
3. Strain the peas into a muslin or thin nylon bag and add the bag to the pan. Let them simmer with the meat and vegetables for a further 1½ hours. Remove from the heat.
4. Remove the bag of peas from the pan and turn them into a basin; add the butter, egg yolks if using, Worcestershire sauce, salt and pepper. Whip very well together and reheat a little if necessary.
5. Place the pork and vegetables on a warm serving dish and add the pease pudding. Serve with English mustard.

From the top: Pickled red cabbage, Cumberland tatie-pot, Boiled pickled pork and pease pudding

DERWENTWATER DUCKLING WITH CUMBERLAND SAUCE

Cumberland sauce can also be served cold with cold duck, chicken, pork and ham. It is worth making in quantity as it keeps well.

1.8 kg (4 lb) duckling
salt
freshly ground black pepper
3 small onions, stuck with 2 cloves each
1 tablespoon butter or oil
2 tablespoons brandy
2 teaspoons cornflour
150 ml ($\frac{1}{4}$ pint) stock (preferably made with the giblets)
Cumberland sauce:
225 g (8 oz) redcurrant jelly
6 tablespoons port wine
grated rind of 1 lemon
1 tablespoon lemon juice
1 tablespoon orange juice
$\frac{1}{2}$ teaspoon made English mustard
watercress sprigs, to garnish

Preparation time: 30 minutes
Cooking time: $1\frac{3}{4}$ hours
Oven: 200°C, 400°F, Gas Mark 6

1. Wipe the duckling all over and sprinkle inside and out with salt and pepper.
2. Put the onions inside the body, then rub the breast and legs with the butter or oil.
3. Roast in the preheated oven for $1\frac{1}{2}$ hours, basting as the fat comes out of the bird. If a lot of fat is released, pour some of it off during cooking. At the end of the cooking time, test that the duckling is ready by piercing the thigh with a skewer. The juices should run clear.
4. Meanwhile, make the Cumberland sauce: bring the redcurrant jelly and the port wine to the boil, reduce the heat and simmer until it is reduced by a quarter.
5. Remove from the heat and add the other ingredients, mix well and bring back to the boil for 2–3 minutes. Set aside.
6. Pour off the excess fat from the roasting pan, leaving only the juices. With the duckling still in the pan, place over a low heat. Warm the brandy in a ladle, pour over and set alight. When the flames die down transfer the duckling to a warmed serving dish and keep warm.
7. Cream the cornflour with a little of the stock, add to the pan juices over a low flame and keep stirring until it is all quite smooth.
8. Add the Cumberland sauce, mixing well and scraping down the sides of the pan. Pour a little over the duck and serve the rest separately.
9. Serve garnished with watercress.

Derwentwater duckling with Cumberland sauce

Hindle wakes chicken

HINDLE WAKES CHICKEN

Hindle Wakes chicken has come down through the ages almost unchanged. The Wake was originally the feast on the eve of the dedication of a church, which subsequently degenerated into a fair with much carousing. The white meat with its black filling and yellow and green garnish looks very medieval.

Serves 4–6
1 chicken, about 2 kg (4½ lb)
1 large onion, sliced
150 ml (¼ pint) vinegar
1 tablespoon brown sugar
Stuffing:
100 g (4 oz) fresh breadcrumbs
225 g (8 oz) prunes, soaked, stoned and chopped
salt
freshly ground black pepper
pinch of ground cinnamon
pinch of ground mace
2 teaspoons dried mixed herbs
1 tablespoon shredded suet or melted butter
2 tablespoons lemon juice
Sauce:
25 g (1 oz) butter
25 g (1 oz) flour
450 ml (¾ pint) chicken stock
1 tablespoon lemon juice
To garnish:
finely grated peel of 2 lemons
12 prunes, stoned
1 lemon, thinly sliced
parsley sprigs
1 tablespoon chopped parsley

Preparation time: 45 minutes
Cooking time: 3½ hours, plus cooling

1. Mix together all the stuffing ingredients very well, then stuff the chicken cavity with this mixture, securing it firmly.
2. Put the stuffed bird into a large saucepan with the sliced onion, seasoning to taste. Barely cover with cold water.
3. Add the vinegar and sugar. Bring to the boil, then lower the heat, cover, and simmer very slowly for about 2½–3 hours. Allow to cool in the broth and skim the top when it is quite cold.
4. When needed, lift the chicken carefully from the saucepan, straining it well, and put on to a large dish. Reserve the stock. Remove all the skin from the bird.
5. To make the sauce, melt the butter in a small saucepan, add the flour and cook for 1 minute.
6. Add the degreased chicken stock, stirring very well until the sauce is smooth and creamy.
7. Add the lemon juice and season to taste. Cook for about 1 minute, then let it cool slightly.
8. Cover the bird with the lemon sauce and sprinkle the lemon peel all over. Leave in a cold place, but not necessarily the refrigerator.
9. Before serving, garnish the bird with the prunes, lemon slices and parsley sprigs, and sprinkle with chopped parsley.

TRIPE AND ONIONS

This is a favourite meal in both Yorkshire and Lancashire where tripe shops used to be as common as fish and chip shops.

Serves 6
1 kg (2 lb) dressed tripe
450 g (1 lb) onions, peeled and sliced
900 ml (1½ pints) milk
50 g (2 oz) butter
50 g (2 oz) plain flour
salt
freshly ground black pepper
pinch of nutmeg

Preparation time: 10 minutes
Cooking time: 2 hours

1. Wash the tripe and cut into 5 cm (2 inch) pieces. Cover with cold water, bring to the boil, then strain off the water.
2. Add the sliced onions and the milk to the tripe, bring to boiling point, being careful not to let the milk boil over. Reduce the heat and simmer for about 1½ hours. Remove the tripe and onions with a slotted spoon and keep warm.
3. In a separate pan melt the butter, then add the flour, mixing well, and cook for 1 minute. Gradually add the milk from the tripe, stirring all the time until a smooth, creamy sauce is obtained. Season to taste, then add the nutmeg.
4. Return the tripe, onions and sauce to the heat, heat through and transfer to a warm serving dish.
Variation: Another method transfers the tripe and onions to a flameproof dish and sprinkles the top with grated Lancashire or Cheshire cheese which is browned lightly under the grill.

PAN HAGGERTY

Pan Haggerty is a Northumberland dish which probably derives its name from the French word *hachis*, meaning 'to chop', as everything in it is either chopped or grated. It is a favourite supper dish.

Serves 4–6
25 g (1 oz) dripping or 2 tablespoons oil
450 g (1 lb) potatoes, peeled and thinly sliced
225 g (8 oz) onions, peeled and thinly sliced
salt
freshly ground black pepper
100 g (4 oz) grated Lancashire cheese

Preparation time: 30 minutes
Cooking time: 35 minutes

1. Heat the dripping or oil in a large frying pan.
2. Place the sliced potatoes over the pan's base, and season to taste. Add the sliced onions, season, and finally add the grated cheese.
3. Cover the pan with a lid and fry gently for 30 minutes.
4. Remove the lid and brown the cheese under the grill. Serve from the pan in the traditional manner.

YORKSHIRE PUDDING

Yorkshire pudding is known all over the Western world, and Yorkshire people maintain that no one but a Yorkshire person can make it. Originally the meat was cooked by hanging it over the fire and the fine drippings were caught in a tin below, to be used subsequently for cooking the pudding. It was served as a first course, sometimes with a drop or two of raspberry vinegar or a little gravy. Yorkshire

From the left: *Tripe and onions, Pan haggerty, Yorkshire pudding*

pudding is not always served with beef in Yorkshire: if with lamb or mutton it is flavoured with chopped mint, or sage with roast pork, and some batter was kept to supply the sweet course with sugar, cinnamon, and either grated apple or currants. Whatever it is served with it must come straight from oven to table.

4 rounded tablespoons plain flour, sifted
½ teaspoon salt
1 egg (size 1), beaten
300 ml (½ pint) milk
cold water
2 tablespoons very hot beef dripping

Preparation time: 15 minutes, plus standing
Cooking time: 35–40 minutes
Oven: 220°C, 425°F, Gas Mark 7

1. Put the flour and salt into a basin and make a well in the centre.
2. Add the beaten egg and half the milk and beat to a smooth paste, for at least 5 minutes.
3. Add the remaining milk and beat again, then thin with cold water to the consistency of thick cream. Leave to stand for about 30 minutes.
4. Have the hot meat dripping ready in a tin about 15 cm (6 inches) square or 4 large separate Yorkshire pudding tins. The fat should be so hot that when the batter is poured in it sizzles.
5. With your fingers, add a few drops of cold water to the batter and stir with a fork.
6. Pour the batter into the hot fat, then place immediately into the preheated oven near the top. For the single pudding, cook for 35–40 minutes, for the smaller ones, 15–20 minutes. Do not open the oven door until the minimum cooking time has elapsed. The pudding should be golden brown and crisp with a creamy but cooked centre.

Variations:

Apple batter pudding: Add sugar to taste and 2 large cooking apples, grated, with a pinch of cinnamon or cloves.

Herb pudding: Add 2 chopped boiled onions and 1 teaspoon dried mixed herbs.

Toad-in-the-hole: Pour the batter over some lightly grilled sausages.

BACON FLODDIES

⸺ ❧ ⸺

Bacon floddies are traditional to Gateshead in County Durham. They can be served on their own but are more usually served with sausages and fried bacon or eggs as a breakfast or supper dish.

225 g (8 oz) potatoes, weighed after peeling
2 medium onions, peeled
175 g (6 oz) bacon rashers, finely chopped
50 g (2 oz) self-raising flour
salt
freshly ground black pepper
2 eggs, beaten
4 tablespoons bacon dripping or oil

Preparation time: 20 minutes
Cooking time: 20 minutes

1. Grate the potatoes and onions into a mixing bowl. Add the finely chopped bacon, the flour and the seasoning and mix very well.
2. Add the eggs, mixing them well through all the ingredients.
3. Heat the dripping in a heavy pan until hot but not smoking. Add tablespoons of the floddies to the pan, not overcrowding them, and fry not too rapidly on both sides until they are golden and cooked through.
4. Drain on paper towels, and keep hot in a dish until ready to serve.

WHITLEY GOOSE

⸺ ❧ ⸺

This is a traditional dish from Whitley Bay in Northumberland, served either as a supper dish with hot, crusty bread or as an accompaniment to hot or cold roast meats. It has nothing to do with geese!

Serves 2
4 medium onions, peeled
100 g (4 oz) Wensleydale or Cheddar cheese, grated
freshly ground black pepper
a little butter
150 ml (¼ pint) single cream

Preparation time: 20 minutes
Cooking time: 30 minutes
Oven: 200°C, 400°F, Gas Mark 6

1. Place the whole peeled onions in a saucepan with water to cover, then boil for about 15 minutes or until they are tender. Strain them and chop coarsely.
2. Mix with half the grated cheese and add pepper to taste.

From the top: Bacon floddies, Whitley goose, Beefsteak pie with cheese crust

3. Lightly butter an ovenproof dish and pour in the cream, then add the onion mixture and sprinkle with the remaining cheese.
4. Put into the preheated oven near the top and bake until it is lightly browned.

BEEFSTEAK PIE WITH CHEESE CRUST

⸺ ❧ ⸺

Besides being eaten on its own with bread, Cheshire cheese is often used in the North for cooking pastry or scones.

Filling:
1 kg (2 lb) lean stewing steak, trimmed and cut into small cubes
2 tablespoons seasoned flour
2 tablespoons dripping or oil
2 medium onions, peeled and finely chopped
4 medium carrots, scraped and finely sliced
pinch of mixed herbs
pinch of ground nutmeg
salt
freshly ground black pepper
2 whole cloves
600 ml (1 pint) beef stock
Pastry:
150 g (5 oz) plain flour, sifted
pinch of salt
60 g (2½ oz) margarine or butter
75 g (3 oz) Cheshire or Lancashire cheese, grated

Preparation time: 30 minutes
Cooking time: 2 hours
Oven: 190°C, 375°F, Gas Mark 5

1. Roll the meat in the seasoned flour. Reserve 2 teaspoons of the excess flour.
2. Heat the fat or oil and just soften the onions and carrots in it but do not let them colour. Remove and put into a flameproof dish.
3. In the same fat quickly brown the meat all over and add it to the vegetables.
4. Add the herbs and spices to the pan juices, together with 2 teaspoons of the seasoned flour. Mix well to absorb the fat, then add the stock and mix well until it boils, and becomes smooth.
5. Pour the thickened stock over the meat and vegetables, bring back to the boil, then cover and put into the preheated oven for about 1–1½ hours or simmer gently on top of the stove.
6. Meanwhile make the crust by putting the flour and salt into a bowl, then rubbing in the fat until it is like coarse breadcrumbs. Add the cheese and mix well.
7. When the meat is cooked, allow to cool slightly, then sprinkle the pastry mix evenly over the meat and bake for about 30 minutes or until it is golden and cooked.

SINGING HINNIES

'Hinny' is a north country term of endearment used to children. Singing hinnies are so-called because the hinny used to be baked on an oiled griddle and its sizzling sound was thought to sound like singing. It is really a fried scone.

225 g (8 oz) plain flour, sifted
pinch of salt
50 g (2 oz) butter
50 g (2 oz) lard
50 g (2 oz) sugar (optional)
75 g (3 oz) currants
1 teaspoon baking powder
2–3 tablespoons milk or sour cream

Preparation time: 30 minutes
Cooking time: 15 minutes

1. Put the flour and salt into a bowl. Rub in the butter and lard until the mixture is like breadcrumbs.
2. Stir in the remaining dry ingredients and mix to a stiff dough with the milk or sour cream.
3. Roll into a ball, then turn out and flatten into a round cake about 1 cm ($\frac{1}{2}$ inch) thick.
4. Heat and lightly grease a pan or griddle. Place the hinny in the pan, prick the top all over and when brown on the bottom, turn over and do the other side.
5. Serve piping hot, cut into wedges, spread liberally with butter.

Variation: Wakes cake is made the same way as the hinny but includes 1 teaspoon caraway seeds and 2 teaspoons grated lemon peel. It is mixed with a lightly beaten egg instead of milk, then rolled out, cut into small rounds, sprinkled with sugar and baked in a 180°C, 350°F, Gas Mark 4 oven for about 15 minutes.

PRESTON GINGERBREAD

This dry, crunchy gingerbread is quite different from the soft gingerbread of the South and is much more like parkin. It is best kept in an airtight tin for 2–3 days before eating.

Serves about 8
350 g (12 oz) plain flour
1 rounded teaspoon ground ginger
pinch of grated nutmeg
pinch of mixed spice
75 g (3 oz) butter, at room temperature
225 g (8 oz) black treacle
1 level teaspoon bicarbonate of soda
5 tablespoons milk, warm
1 egg (size 1), beaten

Preparation time: 30 minutes

Oven: 180°C, 350°F, Gas Mark 4

1. Grease and line a deep tin, 25 × 20 cm (10 × 8 inches).
2. Sift the flour and spices, then rub in the butter until it is like fine breadcrumbs.
3. Warm the treacle gently. Mix the bicarbonate of soda well into the warm milk, add to the treacle.
4. Make a well in the centre of the flour mixture. Pour in the warm mixture together with the beaten egg. Beat the mixture gently but thoroughly.
5. Pour into the prepared tin and bake in the preheated oven for 30–40 minutes or until firm when pressed.
6. Leave to cool in the tin for 5 minutes before turning out on to a wire tray.
7. Leave for a day before cutting.

CUMBERLAND RUM NICKIES

Rum nickies are traditional cakes in Cumbria and there are various recipes. Some omit the dates and use currants flavoured with nutmeg instead, but this recipe, given to me by Mrs. Jean Butterworth, is excellent.

Serves about 6
100 g (4 oz) cooking dates, stoned and chopped
1 tablespoon water
350 g (12 oz) shortcrust pastry, chilled
3 medium cooking apples, peeled and sliced
1 round tablespoon demerara sugar
2 tablespoons rum
50 g (2 oz) butter
a little milk

Preparation time: 30 minutes
Cooking time: 45 minutes
Oven: 200°C, 400°F, Gas Mark 6
then: 180°C, 350°F, Gas Mark 4

1. Put the chopped dates into a saucepan and add the water. Soften them over a low heat, then cool completely.
2. Divide the pastry in half. Roll out one half of the pastry to line a greased 17–20 cm (7–8 inch) shallow pie plate.
3. Place the sliced apples on the pastry and scatter the sugar over them.
4. Mix the rum with the butter into the dates and spread over the apples, then roll out the remaining pastry for a lid, dampening the edges and pressing them down.
5. Lightly prick over the top with a fork, brush with milk and bake in the preheated oven for 15 minutes, then reduce the oven temperature and continue cooking for a further 15 minutes or until the top is golden brown.
6. Serve cut into wedges, hot or cold, with lightly whipped cream.

From the top, clockwise: *Singing hinnies, Cumberland rum nickies, Preston gingerbread*

SIMNEL CAKE

Nowadays, Simnel cake is usually made at Easter, but originally it was made for the fourth Sunday in Lent, known as 'Mothering Sunday', when servant girls and boys were given one day off to visit their mothers and to take them a cake. The name Simnel comes from *Siminellus*, a Roman festive bread eaten during the Spring fertility rites, while the eleven marzipan balls on top represent the Apostles, omitting Judas Iscariot: a fine example of the combination of pagan and Christian festive rites.

Serves 10–12
350 g (12 oz) currants
100 g (4 oz) sultanas
75 g (3 oz) candied peel, chopped
225 g (8 oz) flour, sifted
pinch of salt
1 teaspoon ground cinnamon
1 teaspoon ground nutmeg
175 g (6 oz) butter or margarine
175 g (6 oz) caster sugar
3 eggs, beaten
a little milk to mix
2 tablespoons apricot jam, warmed
Almond paste:
175 g (6 oz) icing sugar, sifted
175 g (6 oz) caster sugar
350 g (12 oz) ground almonds
few drops of almond essence
2 eggs, lightly beaten
1 teaspoon lemon juice
cornflour, for sprinkling

Preparation time: about 30 minutes
Cooking time: 2½–3 hours
Oven: 160°C, 325°F, Gas Mark 3

1. To make the almond paste, sift the icing sugar into a mixing bowl and add the caster sugar and almonds.
2. Add the almond essence, eggs and lemon juice and make a stiff mixture with your hands.
3. Form into a ball and turn out on to a surface covered with a scattering of icing sugar mixed with a little cornflour. Knead lightly and set aside.
4. Grease and line an 18 cm (7 inch) cake tin.
5. Divide the almond paste into 3. Roll 2 of the portions into circles the size of the cake tin.
6. Mix together the fruit and peel with a tablespoon of the flour. Sift the rest of the flour, salt and spices into a bowl.
7. Cream the fat and sugar until pale and fluffy, then add the eggs a little at a time, beating well after each addition.
8. Fold in half the flour and fruit with a metal spoon, then add the remainder.
9. Pour in just enough milk to make a fairly stiff consistency and mix well.
10. Put half the cake mixture into the prepared tin, smooth over and cover with 1 round of almond paste. Then lay the remaining cake mixture on top and level off the surface.
11. Bake in the preheated oven for about 2 hours, or until cooked through. (Test with a small skewer – if it comes out clean, the cake is ready.) Allow to cool in the tin.
12. Meanwhile, from the remaining almond paste make 11 small balls to represent the Apostles.
13. When the cake is cool, turn out, brush with apricot jam and lay the second round of almond paste on top. Fix the 'Apostles' round the edge with dabs of apricot jam or beaten egg.
14. Brush the cake with any remaining egg or jam and brown lightly under the grill, if liked.

YORKSHIRE CURD TARTS

Makes about 12 tarts

100 g (4 oz) butter or margarine, at room
temperature
225 g (8 oz) plain flour, sifted
1 tablespoon caster sugar
pinch of salt
1 egg yolk
1–2 tablespoons cold water
225 g (8 oz) fresh curd or cottage cheese, sieved
50 g (2 oz) caster sugar
1 teaspoon grated lemon rind
2 eggs, separated
2 tablespoons currants or sultanas
1 tablespoon butter, melted
pinch of nutmeg

Preparation time: 30 minutes
Cooking time: 35 minutes
Oven: 220°C, 425°F, Gas Mark 7
then: 180°C, 350°F, Gas Mark 4

1. First make the pastry by rubbing the fat into the flour, adding the sugar, salt and egg yolk and mixing well. Finally add the cold water to make a firm dough.
2. Turn out on to a floured surface and knead well, then roll into a ball and chill for at least 30 minutes.
3. Mix together all the remaining ingredients except the egg whites.
4. Roll out the pastry. Either line 12 greased deep patty tins or a 20–22 cm (8–9 inch) greased flat tin with the pastry; lightly prick over the bottom.
5. Beat the egg whites stiffly, and lightly but thoroughly fold into the cheese mixture.
6. Divide between the patty tin cases, or spread over the large flan and cook in the preheated oven for 10 minutes, then reduce the oven temperature and continue cooking for a further 20–25 minutes or until the cheese mixture is set and golden.

From the top: *Simnel cake, Yorkshire curd tarts*

ECCLES CAKES

These little cakes evolved from Puritan days when rich Christmas cakes and puddings were banned. A clever baker at Eccles thought up these little cakes as an alternative and they have continued to be made through the ages.

Makes about 14
450 g (1 lb) frozen puff pastry, thawed
175 g (6 oz) currants
25 g (1 oz) butter, at room temperature
40 g (1½ oz) soft brown sugar
25 g (1 oz) mixed peel, chopped
pinch of nutmeg
1 egg white, lightly beaten
caster sugar, to sprinkle

Preparation time: 45 minutes
Cooking time: 20 minutes
Oven: 220°C, 425°F, Gas Mark 7

1. Roll out the pastry thinly and cut into 10 cm (4 inch) rounds.
2. Mix well all the other ingredients, except the egg white and caster sugar, and put a heaped teaspoonful on each round.
3. Dampen the edges, gather them together in the centre and pinch to seal.
4. Turn the rounds over and very gently roll them out just until the fruit begins to show through the pastry.
5. Put on to a dampened baking tray and score twice across the surface. Brush lightly with the egg white and sprinkle with caster sugar.
6. Bake in the preheated oven for 20 minutes or until golden brown.

CUMBERLAND RUM BUTTER

This is traditional to both Cumberland and Westmorland. Rum butter is eaten with scones, on steamed puddings, and especially with mince pies and Christmas pudding.

450 g (1 lb) dark Barbados sugar, or soft brown sugar
1 teaspoon grated nutmeg
4–5 tablespoons dark rum
225 g (8 oz) unsalted butter

Preparation time: 20 minutes

1. Mix together the sugar, nutmeg and rum.
2. Melt the butter but do not allow it to colour. Pour over the sugar mixture and mix well.
3. Put into small bowls or dishes, and cover tightly. Keep cool until needed.

CUMBRIAN LEMON CAKE

The first Englishmen to enjoy oranges and lemons were the Crusaders, who wintered with Richard Coeur de Lion in Jaffa in 1191–2.

Serves about 6
100 g (4 oz) butter, at room temperature
50 g (2 oz) lard
150 g (5 oz) caster sugar
2 eggs (size 1)
225 g (8 oz) self-raising flour
2 tablespoons lemon juice
grated rind of 1 lemon
50 g (2 oz) candied lemon peel, chopped
1 tablespoon milk (optional)
To serve:
icing sugar for sprinkling
lemon curd

From the top:
Cumbrian lemon cake,
Eccles cakes

Preparation time: 25 minutes
Cooking time: 1–1½ hours
Oven: 180°C, 350°F, Gas Mark 4

1. First lightly butter an 18 cm (7 inch) cake tin with a removable base.
2. Cream the butter, lard and sugar until light and fluffy. Add the eggs singly together with about 1 tablespoon of flour for each and mix in thoroughly. Fold in the rest of the flour.
3. Add the lemon juice, the finely grated rind and the chopped candied lemon peel. Mix well, and only add the milk if the mixture seems too stiff. It should be of firm, dropping consistency.
4. Pour into the prepared tin and bake in the centre of the preheated oven for about 1 hour. Check that it is cooked through by inserting a small skewer, which will come out clean if the cake is ready. If necessary, continue cooking for up to a further 30 minutes.
5. Leave to cool in the tin for 5 minutes before removing and cooling on a wire tray.
6. To serve, the cake can either be sprinkled with sifted icing sugar or cut across and spread with lemon curd, but it is also extremely good eaten just as it is.

DAMSON FOOL WITH MACAROONS

Cheshire and Cumbria are famous for their damsons, especially the Lyth Valley area, where they are large, juicy and much sweeter than damsons grown elsewhere. Lyth Valley damsons are often eaten raw, like grapes, with Lancashire cheese. Locally they are called Witherslack damsons.

Serves 4–6
750 g (1½ lb) damsons
175 g (6 oz) sugar, or to taste
½ teaspoon lemon juice
450 ml (¾ pint) double or whipping cream, whipped
2 egg whites, stiffly beaten
Macaroons:
2 egg whites, stiffly beaten
100 g (4 oz) caster sugar
75 g (3 oz) ground almonds
1 teaspoon vanilla essence
rice paper

Preparation time: 1 hour
Cooking time: 40 minutes
Oven: 160°C, 325°F, Gas Mark 3

1. First make the macaroons by putting the stiffly beaten egg whites in a bowl then adding the other ingredients and folding them in thoroughly.
2. Lay the rice paper on a baking sheet and pipe or spoon the mixture on to it in mounds about 2.5 cm (1 inch) across.
3. Put into the centre of the preheated oven and bake for 20–30 minutes until they are set and golden brown.
4. Lift the macaroons off when cooked and cool on a wire tray.
5. Put the damsons into a saucepan with the sugar and lemon and enough water just to cover. Simmer until soft. Leave until they are cool enough, then lift them out and remove the stones. Then blend in the liquidizer and turn in to a large bowl.
6. Fold two-thirds of the whipped cream and all the egg white lightly but thoroughly into the damsons, seeing that you get right down to the bottom and that the mixture is an even colour.
7. Transfer the mixture to a serving bowl, decorate the top with the almond macaroons, and dot all over with the remaining whipped cream.
Variation: Gooseberries are also very popular in the north and can be made into a fool the same way as the damsons. The macaroons are optional.

SUMMER PUDDING

This was a popular pudding in the spa towns where it was known sometimes as 'Hydropathic pudding', because it was served in those establishments where pastry was thought to be heavy and indigestible.

Serves 6
10 slices of crustless white bread, not too fresh
3 tablespoons milk
750 g (1½ lb) mixed soft fruit (raspberries, redcurrants or white currants, strawberries and cherries if available)
100 g (4 oz) caster sugar
a little fresh fruit to decorate, if liked
single cream, to serve

Preparation time: 40 minutes, plus pressing
Cooking time: 5 minutes

1. Lightly butter a pudding basin of 1 litre (1¾ pint) capacity.
2. Moisten the bread with the milk.
3. Hull, stone, or top and tail the fruit as necessary. Cook it all very gently with the sugar for 4–5 minutes until the sugar melts and the juices run. Spoon off a few spoonfuls of juice as it cools and reserve.
4. Line the sides and bottom of the basin with the bread slices, cutting where necessary and checking there are no spaces. Reserve enough bread slices for the lid.
5. Pour in the fruit, which should come almost to the top. Cover closely with the remaining bread.
6. Put a small plate over the top (it should just fit inside the rim of the basin), and weight it with something heavy. Leave to press overnight in a cool place.
7. To serve, remove the weight and the plate. Place a serving plate over the top and reverse quickly so the pudding comes out easily in one piece.
8. Pour the remaining juices slowly all over the pudding, especially over those places where the juices might not have seeped through thoroughly.
9. Keep cold until ready to serve. Decorate with a few pieces of fresh fruit, if liked and serve with single cream.

From the top: *Damson fool with Macaroons, Summer pudding*

WALES

Wales, a land of mountains, mists, and sea coast, with a people who have always clung to their traditions and refused to become part of England, retains a unique traditional cookery as well as a language.

Nowadays, it will be very difficult to find traditional Welsh cooking in Cardiff or in the big seaside resorts such as Llandudno or Colwyn Bay, unless a brave, enthusiastic and enterprising hotel or restaurant decides to specialise in Welsh food. However, manuscripts and notebooks from castles and great houses in Wales have been handed down to us and some of the traditional Welsh dishes are as well known today as they were in the past. In the deep country, if you fall into conversation with an elderly Welsh farmer or his wife, you may be told about the dishes that were made almost a hundred years ago and may be made today, with some modifications.

Welsh sheep are small and have a particularly delicious flavour when eaten as lamb. One very old farmer recently described a dinner where the four joints, legs and shoulders, of a lamb were cooked on a spit with every now and again thyme and rosemary being sprinkled over them. In the tray underneath the spit, home-made sausages were sizzling. On the fire a saucepan of young turnips boiled. There had been three visiting couples, his brother and brother-in-law and a friend and all the wives. His own wife was the cook and she put plenty of butter and pepper with the turnips. When they sat down to table, each couple shared a leg or a shoulder and they ate up all four joints, which would probably have weighed about $1\frac{1}{4}$ kg ($2\frac{1}{2}$ lb) each and all the sausages and turnips. The wives didn't eat quite as much as their husbands, he said, but they didn't do badly! This was a dinner which had been remembered for more than 50 years (the old gentleman was in his late seventies when he described it). The lamb had been bred on his farm, the sausages made from a recent pig-killing and the turnips and the butter were also from the farm.

Anyone who can afford to take a few days off work and drive to any unfrequented part of Wales can then wander among the farms and villages, and stay at small inns or farmhouses. He or she may still find that the homegrown, traditionally cooked food which is rarely seen in the cities is offered. And more will be offered if an interest in the local produce is shown.

Welsh farm butter and cheese are still made today and sold in small quantities in shops throughout Wales. Some of the local cheeses, for example, Caerphilly, are particularly delicious with very succulent flavours.

Conway Castle, Wales

51

CABBAGE AND LEEK SOUP

When not on shift, many Welsh miners enjoy working in the open air on their allotments or cottage gardens. Almost all grow leeks and cabbages, so this fresh, green soup could almost be called 'Miner's Soup'. In fact, it is also made on Welsh farms and in manor houses, while the town housewife buys the vegetables and makes it in the same way.

Serves 6
1.2 litres (2 pints) chicken stock
8 leeks, trimmed, washed and chopped into 2 cm
($\frac{3}{4}$ inch) pieces
1.25 kg (2$\frac{1}{2}$ lb) green or Savoy cabbage, hard stalks
and outer leaves removed, and chopped into 2 cm
($\frac{3}{4}$ inch) pieces
1 large onion, peeled and finely sliced
salt
freshly ground black pepper
To garnish:
6 slices of toast, each cut into 12 squares (optional)
75 g (3 oz) grated Cheddar cheese (optional)

Preparation time: 10 minutes
Cooking time: 50 minutes

1. In a large saucepan, bring the stock to the boil.
2. Drop in all the vegetables. Bring back to the boil, then cover and simmer for 45 minutes, stirring occasionally.
3. Add salt and pepper to taste.
4. Ladle into 6 bowls, allowing enough vegetables in each to show just above the surface of the liquid.
5. The soup can be served just as it is, or each bowl can be garnished with 12 squares of toast, sprinkled with 15 g ($\frac{1}{2}$ oz) grated Cheddar cheese.

COLD LEEK AND POTATO SOUP

Serves 8
6 leeks, washed and finely sliced
2 small onions, peeled and finely chopped
25 g (1 oz) butter
3 large potatoes, about 175 g (6 oz) each, peeled and
sliced
1.2 litres (2 pints) chicken stock (can be made with
stock cubes)
salt
600 ml (1 pint) milk
freshly ground black pepper
300 ml ($\frac{1}{2}$ pint) double or whipping cream, whipped
until it just holds a peak
2 tablespoons chopped chives, to garnish

Preparation time: 15 minutes, plus chilling
Cooking time: 45 minutes

1. Fry the leeks and onions in the butter over a gentle heat until translucent but not brown.
2. Add the potatoes, the chicken stock and 1 teaspoon of salt and boil for 30–35 minutes.
3. Put the mixture in a blender or through a sieve and return it to the heat.
4. Add the milk. Season with salt and pepper, increase the heat and bring the mixture just to the boil.
5. Remove from the heat, cool and then chill in the refrigerator for at least 2 hours.
6. Fold in the whipped cream, sprinkle with chopped chives and serve immediately.

STUFFED MUSHROOMS (COLD)

This recipe comes from Holywell in North Wales. Delicious and slightly unusual, it tastes best of all made with home-picked field mushrooms, but is still very good with the shop-bought varieties.

8 medium or 12 small mushrooms, washed and stalks
trimmed
butter to fry
Green butter filling:
1 spinach leaf
3 sprigs parsley
2 sprigs mint
2 sage leaves (optional)
75 g (3 oz) butter
pinch of salt

Preparation time: 15 minutes, plus chilling
Cooking time: 5 minutes

1. In a heavy-bottomed frying pan, fry the mushrooms in the butter very lightly, until just soft.
2. Drain the mushrooms, cool and chill slightly.
3. Meanwhile, make the green butter filling. Finely chop the spinach and fresh herbs, or pass them together through a parsley chopper.
4. Mix the chopped herbs into the butter with a wooden spoon, beating well. Add the salt.
5. Lay the mushrooms, stalks uppermost, on a serving dish. Pipe the green butter around and over the stalks, or simply spread neatly.
6. Chill for 1 hour or more, before serving.

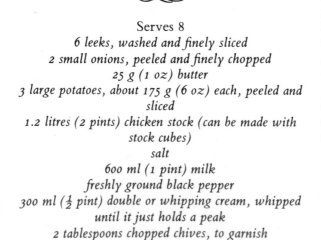

CRAB IN CREAM SAUCE

A very good hot starter. Crabs used to be so plentiful around the Welsh coast that, in great houses and castles, several different ways of serving them were invented, in case family and guests should tire of them.

50 g (2 oz) butter
25 g (1 oz) plain flour
175 ml (6 fl oz) milk
½ teaspoon ground mace
¼ teaspoon salt
¼ teaspoon pepper
225 g (8 oz) fresh or frozen crab meat
2 tablespoons double cream
50 g (2 oz) fresh white breadcrumbs
1 tablespoon grated Parmesan cheese

Preparation time: 10 minutes
Cooking time: 20 minutes
Oven: 200°C, 400°F, Gas Mark 6

1. Melt 25 g (1 oz) of the butter in a heavy 900 ml (1½ pint) saucepan. Stir in the flour and amalgamate well. Slowly stir in the milk and boil gently to make a smooth, thick sauce.
2. Stir in the mace, salt and pepper. Mix in all the crab and bring just to the boil. Stir in the cream and check the seasoning.
3. Pour into 4 small, buttered ovenproof dishes and sprinkle each with breadcrumbs and then Parmesan cheese. The dishes can wait in the refrigerator for several hours before cooking.
4. Dot the top of each dish with the remaining butter and stand the small dishes in 1 cm (½ inch) of water in a baking tray. Bake for 10 minutes in a preheated oven. The tops should be crisp and golden brown and the crab thick and creamy.

From the bottom, clockwise: *Cold leek and potato soup, Cabbage and leek soup, Crab in cream sauce, Stuffed mushrooms*

From the top:
*Fisherman's stew from
the Gower peninsula,
Trout wrapped in bacon*

TROUT WRAPPED IN BACON

This way of cooking trout has been traditional
on Welsh farms for three hundred years and
probably much longer. Home-cured bacon and
fresh-caught trout probably made an
even better dish.

*50 g (2 oz) butter
4 medium trout, cleaned
2 sprigs tarragon, chopped
2 sprigs marjoram, chopped
4 tablespoons finely chopped onions or chives
1 teaspoon freshly ground black pepper
8 long rashers smoked streaky bacon
2 tablespoons finely chopped fresh parsley*

Preparation time: 10 minutes
Cooking time: 8–10 minutes

1. Put a quarter of the butter in the cavity of each
fish and press into it a quarter of the chopped herbs
except the parsley. Sprinkle $\frac{1}{4}$ teaspoon of black
pepper into each.
2. Using scissors, cut the rind from the bacon
rashers. Wind 2 rashers spirally round each fish,
starting where the head joins the body and
finishing at the tail fin.
3. Lay the fish on a grill pan, heads facing the
same way, and cook under a pre-heated, very hot
grill for 3–4 minutes. If the bacon begins to burn,
lower the pan a little, but not the heat. After 3
minutes turn the trout and cook for 3 minutes on
the other side. Test with a skewer for doneness.
4. Serve sprinkled with chopped parsley.

FISHERMAN'S STEW FROM THE GOWER PENINSULA

Traditionally, this dish made a good supper for
Welsh fishermen who would bring home some
of the catch in the morning to their wives, go
to bed and get up at tea time to find a hot stew.

Serves 6
*1.2 litres (2 pints) cockles, scrubbed and soaked in
cold water or frozen cockles
3 medium onions
bouquet garni
$\frac{1}{2}$ teaspoon mace
salt
pepper
2 chicken stock cubes
300 ml ($\frac{1}{2}$ pint) white wine
450 g (1 lb) haddock fillets, skinned
450 g (1 lb) plaice fillets, skinned
50 g (2 oz) butter
50 g (2 oz) plain flour
225 g (8 oz) crab meat
225 g (8 oz) shrimps or prawns, shelled
1 teaspoon saffron*

Preparation time: 20 minutes, plus soaking
Cooking time: 1 hour 20 minutes

1. Strain the cockles, put in a large pan with 1.75
litres (3 pints) of water and bring to the boil. As
soon as they open, take the pan from the heat and
reserve the liquor. Using a teaspoon, remove the
cockles from the shell, and set aside.

2. Strain the liquor in which the cockles were cooked and add one of the onions, peeled and quartered, the bouquet garni, mace and a little salt and pepper. Bring to the boil, and reduce by one third by boiling briskly for 30 minutes.

3. If frozen cockles are used, add one of the onions, the bouquet garni, mace, salt and pepper to 1.25 litres (2 pints) of water, stir in 2 chicken stock cubes and bring to the boil.

4. Add the white wine and the remaining onions, finely chopped.

5. Slide the haddock fillets into the liquid over the onions and then the plaice fillets on top of all.

6. Poach very gently for 30 minutes. Then lift out the plaice fillets with a fish slice, cut each one in half and keep warm. Take out the haddock fillets, flake the flesh and set on one side.

7. Melt the butter in a large pan, add the flour and cook, stirring well for 2 minutes. Slowly stir the broth into it and simmer for 5 minutes until it thickens.

8. Return the flaked haddock to the broth, add the crab meat, the shrimps or prawns, the cockles and a good pinch of saffron. Simmer for 2–3 minutes and adjust the seasoning as necessary.

9. Return the plaice fillets to the pan and serve immediately.

BAKED SALMON

Serves 6
1 salmon, about 2 kg (4½ lb)
1 tablespoon flour
salt
pepper
50 g (2 oz) butter
1 sprig tarragon
1 bay leaf
75 g (3 oz) Green butter (page 52), chilled

Preparation time: 20 minutes plus chilling
Cooking time: 35–45 minutes
Oven: 180°C, 350°F, Gas Mark 4

1. Sprinkle the salmon inside and out with the flour, salt and pepper.

2. Butter a large sheet of aluminium foil and lay the salmon on it. Put the herbs on the fish and dot with the rest of the butter. Wrap up firmly.

3. Lay the parcel on a baking tray and bake in a preheated oven for 30–35 minutes. Open the parcel and insert a skewer to see if the fish is cooked. If not, cook for another 10 minutes.

4. When cooked, unwrap the fish and lay it on a flat, ovenproof dish. Put flat cakes of chilled Green butter along the fish and return it to the oven for 2 minutes. Serve at once. The butter should be running down the sides of the salmon.

PURÉE OF SPINACH

25 g (1 oz) butter
1 kg (2 lb) fresh spinach, washed
50 g (2 oz) double cream (optional)
3 tablespoons milk
1 teaspoon lemon juice
salt
black pepper

Preparation time: 5 minutes
Cooking time: 10 minutes

1. Melt the butter in a heavy saucepan, put in the spinach, turn well, cover and cook for 3 minutes.

2. Stir uncovered for a further 2 minutes then process in a blender.

3. Stir in the cream, if using, and add the milk to thin it to a pouring consistency. Add the lemon juice, salt and pepper to taste.

Baked salmon

LEEKS WITH CHEESE SAUCE

The leek is the Welsh national vegetable. This is a very good supper dish, often served with sausages and bacon rolls.

Serves 4–6
8 leeks, washed and cut in 2.5 cm (1 inch) lengths
40 g (1½ oz) butter
25 g (1 oz) flour
salt
300 ml (½ pint) milk
75 g (3 oz) grated cheese
1 tablespoon breadcrumbs

Preparation time: 10 minutes
Cooking time: 30 minutes
Oven: 230°C, 450°F, Gas Mark 8

1. Put the prepared leeks into boiling, salted water and cook for 20 minutes or until tender.
2. Meanwhile, make the cheese sauce. Melt 25 g (1 oz) of the butter in a small, heavy saucepan, and stir in the flour until it has taken up all the butter, but do not allow to colour. Add the salt and half the milk, stirring all the time. Put in the grated cheese and stir until it has melted and thoroughly combined. Finally add the remaining milk, a little at a time, until the sauce is smooth.
3. Drain the leeks, reserving some of the water in which they cooked.
4. Stir 2 tablespoons of the water in which the leeks have cooked into the cheese sauce and mix hard for a few seconds.
5. Pour half the leeks into an ovenproof dish, pour half the sauce over them, then put in the remaining leeks and the remainder of the sauce.
6. Sprinkle the top with breadcrumbs and dot with the remaining butter.
7. Stand the dish in a tin with a little hot water in it and bake in a preheated oven for about 10 minutes.

LAVERBREAD

When picked from the rocks at low tide, laver seaweed is almost purple in colour. When cooked, it is a dark, bright green. It is picked round the coasts of Wales and the West coast of Scotland and eaten mainly in Wales, though its use is spreading as it can nowadays be bought canned or dried in many supermarkets or health food shops. If fresh picked, the laver has to be washed in at least two lots of fresh water, then drained and boiled in plenty more fresh water for about 20 minutes. Then it is drained again, so that a green, almost spinach-like mass remains, the true laverbread.

It is sold fresh in buckets, ready to chop or purée for sauces. Orange juice added to the purée brings out the characteristic flavour and makes a superb sauce for salmon or duck. However, its simplest use is in Laverbread cakes, traditionally served with bacon for breakfast.

LAVERBREAD CAKES

Serves 4–6
450 g (1 lb) laverbread
100 g (4 oz) fine oatmeal
6 back rashers smoked bacon

Preparation time: 5 minutes
Cooking time: 8 minutes

1. Mix the laverbread and the oatmeal and form into little cakes, about 5 cm (2 inch) across and 2 cm (¾ inch) thick. Flatten and shape them with a palette knife.
2. Fry the bacon rashers and keep warm.
3. Drop the laver cakes into the hot bacon fat and fry fairly fast for 2 minutes on each side, shaping and patting the cakes as they fry.
4. Lift out carefully with a palette knife or slice and serve with the bacon rashers.

WELSH RAREBIT

Welsh Rarebit (generally pronounced 'rabbit') is served world-wide. Adding beer improves the dish.

50 g (2 oz) butter
225 g (8 oz) Cheddar cheese, grated
salt
pepper
1 teaspoon mustard (optional)

2 tablespoons beer (optional)
4 slices of bread, toasted

Preparation time: 4 minutes
Cooking time: 8 minutes

1. Melt the butter in a heavy saucepan, stir in the cheese, add salt and pepper, and mustard if liked. Stir over a gentle heat until the cheese melts.
2. This mixture may be used as it is, or can be bound with the egg yolks if the butter and cheese show signs of separating. The beer should be stirred in last, if using.
3. Spread the toast slices with the mixture and brown under a preheated grill for 3–4 minutes.

From the bottom, clockwise: Welsh rarebit, Laverbread cakes, Leeks with cheese sauce

SALT DUCK

—————— ✀ ——————

Salt duck has an inimitable flavour, not very salt but very fresh and appetizing. The sauce is very important, as it supplements the flavour. In Wales, laverbread and orange sauce is preferred, but the duck is also very good with a spinach purée or with a sauce of orange and port wine.

———————————————

1 large duck, about 1.5–1.75 kg (3½–4 lb)
225 g (8 oz) sea salt

———————————————

Preparation time: 20 minutes, plus marinating
Cooking time: 2 hours
Oven: 180°C, 350°F, Gas Mark 4
then: 230°C, 450°F, Gas Mark 8

———————————————

1. Buy the duck and the salt 2 days before the bird is to be cooked and served.
2. Rub the duck all over, outside and in, with about a quarter of the salt and put it on a flat dish in the refrigerator. Repeat the process in the evening, twice on the following day and once on the morning on which it is to be cooked.
3. Lift the duck and rinse it well, inside and out, under cold, running water. Pat with paper towels.
4. Put the bird in a deep casserole only a little larger than the duck, and just cover with water. Stand the casserole in a baking tin also filled with water and place both in a preheated, moderate oven for 1½ hours.
5. After this time, remove the duck. Place it in a baking tin only. Raise the oven heat and return the duck to the oven for about 30 minutes to crisp the skin.
6. Serve on a large flat dish with one of the following sauces poured all round it.

From the top, clockwise: *Purée of spinach (page 55), Orange and port wine sauce, Salt duck with Laverbread and orange sauce*

LAVERBREAD AND ORANGE SAUCE

—————— ✀ ——————

225 g (8 oz) prepared laverbread, fresh or canned
600 ml (1 pint) chicken stock
8 tablespoons orange juice
¼ teaspoon ground mace
½ teaspoon sugar
1 tablespoon cornflour (optional)

———————————————

Preparation time: 5 minutes
Cooking time: 30 minutes

———————————————

1. Boil the laverbread in the chicken stock for 20 minutes.
2. Mix together the orange juice, mace and sugar.
3. Stir the laverbread into the orange mixture and put through a sieve or food mill.
4. The purée can be thickened if preferred. Mix the cornflour with a little cold water in a bowl. Bring the purée to the boil and stir a little into the cornflour. Pour the cornflour mixture back into the purée and stir hard for 2 minutes, until the sauce is the consistency of thin cream.

ORANGE AND PORT WINE SAUCE

—————— ✀ ——————

25 g (1 oz) butter
25 g (1 oz) plain flour
300 ml (½ pint) brown stock
2 tablespoons orange juice
1 teaspoon grated orange zest
150 ml (¼ pint) port
¼ teaspoon freshly ground black pepper
¼ teaspoon redcurrant jelly
salt

———————————————

Preparation time: 5 minutes
Cooking time: 8 minutes

———————————————

1. Melt the butter in a saucepan, add the flour and stir well to make a roux. Add the stock and stir until the sauce is thick and smooth.
2. Stir in the orange juice, zest, port and pepper.
3. Add the redcurrant jelly and stir until it is melted. Add salt to taste.

LOIN OF LAMB, ROLLED AND STUFFED

This way of serving loin of lamb is generally reserved for special occasions. The fine flavour of Welsh lamb is emphasized by the herbs and stuffing and the dish is easy to serve, as the meat is carved in advance. Glazed carrots make a delicious and decorative accomplishment.

Serves 4–6
1.5 kg (3½ lb) loin of lamb, boned, with bones reserved for stock
1 bouquet garni
40 g (1½ oz) seasoned flour
3 tablespoons breadcrumbs, lightly browned in a frying pan
2–3 tablespoons soft margarine, dripping or cooking fat
Stuffing:
2 tablespoons finely chopped onion
25 g (1 oz) butter
5 tablespoons fresh white breadcrumbs
1 tablespoon chopped parsley
½ tablespoon chopped chives
½ tablespoon chopped mint
1 teaspoon grated orange rind
salt
pepper
2 tablespoons orange juice
1 egg, beaten
Sauce:
1 onion, peeled and sliced
1 teaspoon flour
300 ml (½ pint) stock, made from the lamb bones
1 tablespoon redcurrant jelly
salt
pepper
1 tablespoon orange juice

Preparation time: 30 minutes
Cooking time: 1¾ hours
Oven: 200°C, 400°F, Gas Mark 6

1. If the joint is rolled and tied, undo it and lay the meat out flat. Put the bones on to boil in 1 litre (1¾ pints) salted water with a bouquet garni.
2. Prepare the stuffing. Cook the onion in the butter until soft but not browned. Stir it into the breadcrumbs and then add the parsley, chives, mint, orange rind, salt and pepper. Stir well together and bind with orange juice and some of the beaten egg.
3. Spread the stuffing over the inside of the meat, then roll up and tie securely with string.
4. Spread the seasoned flour on a plate and the browned breadcrumbs on another. Roll the joint in the flour, then brush with the remaining beaten egg and roll in the crumbs until the whole of the outside is coated.

5. Heat the margarine in a roasting tin. Put in the joint, baste immediately and roast in a preheated oven for 1¼–1½ hours.
6. Just before the joint is cooked, remove the bone stock from the heat and strain it.
7. Place the joint on a dish and keep hot.
8. Make the sauce. Fry the sliced onion in a little fat from the roasting tin until it is softened and just turning brown. Sprinkle in the flour, add 300 ml (½ pint) of the stock and the redcurrant jelly, bring to the boil and boil briskly for 2 minutes. Add the seasoning and sharpen with the orange juice. Remove from the heat and strain.
9. Carve the meat into 1 cm (½ inch) slices and lay it on a preheated dish. Spoon over a little of the sauce, and serve the rest separately.

From the top: Glazed carrots, Loin of lamb, rolled and stuffed

GLAZED CARROTS

12 carrots, of roughly equal size, scraped
50 g (2 oz) butter
50 g (2 oz) sugar

Preparation time: 2 minutes
Cooking time: 20 minutes

1. Cook the carrots in 1 litre (1¾ pints) of boiling, salted water until just tender and drain.
2. Melt the butter in the saucepan, return the carrots to the pan and sprinkle over the sugar.
3. Cook over medium heat, turning the carrots until coated with the butter and sugar.

BOILED LEG OF LAMB WITH CAPER SAUCE

—— ❧ ——

Boiled lamb or mutton is not often served now, even in Wales. Yet it is extremely good when a small, lean leg of young Welsh lamb is used, together with caper sauce which works magic on the delicate flavour of the meat.

Serves 8–10
1 leg of lamb or mutton, 1.5–2.25 kg (3–5 lb)
1 head of celery, sliced
1 leek, washed and cut into chunks
2 carrots, scraped and sliced
4 medium onions, peeled and halved
2 cloves
1 sprig thyme
1 sprig parsley
1 bay leaf
1 tablespoon salt
pepper
Sauce:
25 g (1 oz) butter
25 g (1 oz) plain flour
300 ml ($\frac{1}{2}$ pint) stock in which the lamb has been simmering
salt
pepper
300 ml ($\frac{1}{2}$ pint) milk
2 tablespoons lemon juice
50 g (2 oz) capers
15 g ($\frac{1}{2}$ oz) chopped parsley

Preparation time: 20 minutes
Cooking time: 2–2$\frac{1}{2}$ hours

1. Saw the end bone off the leg and tie the joint well with string to hold it in shape. Put it in a large pot, cover it with water and add the prepared vegetables and herbs, salt and pepper.
2. Bring to the boil and remove the scum carefully as it rises to the surface.
3. Simmer for 2–2$\frac{1}{2}$ hours, until cooked. Test by pricking the meat with a skewer in the thick part; if the juice runs clear, it is done.
4. Fifteen minutes before the lamb is cooked, pour off 300 ml ($\frac{1}{2}$ pint) of the cooking liquid.
5. Melt the butter in a pan and add the flour, stirring. Cook without allowing it to colour.
6. Add the boiling stock gradually, stirring all the time. Season to taste with salt and pepper.
7. Add the milk and simmer for 5 minutes.
8. Just before serving, add the lemon juice and the capers. Stir the lemon juice in slowly, a few drops at a time, to avoid curdling. Add a sprinkling of chopped parsley.
9. Lift the lamb out of the pot, draining off all liquid, cut off the string and place it on a large, warm serving dish. Pour half the sauce over the joint and serve the remainder in a sauceboat.

LOIN OF PORK WITH CABBAGE CAKE FROM THE WELSH MARCHES

—— ❧ ——

This was a traditional dish among cottagers after pig-killing. The loin was considered a delicacy and cabbages and apples were freely available from the garden.

Serves 6
1.5 kg (3$\frac{1}{2}$ lb) loin of pork, chined and scored
2 tablespoons flour
salt
1 tablespoon dripping or cooking fat
300 ml ($\frac{1}{2}$ pint) stock, made from the pork bone or from a stock cube
Cabbage cake:
1 white cabbage, about 1 kg (2 lb), very finely shredded
25 g (1 oz) butter
1 medium onion, peeled and very finely chopped
50 g (2 oz) sultanas
salt
pepper
4 medium eating apples, peeled and quartered
To garnish:
1 tablespoon finely chopped parsley
2 hard-boiled eggs, shelled and quartered

Preparation time: 30 minutes
Cooking time: 1$\frac{1}{2}$ hours
Oven: 200°C, 400°F, Gas Mark 6

1. Rub the pork with flour and salt and place in a hot baking tin in the preheated oven, with a tablespoon of dripping or cooking fat. Cook for 1$\frac{1}{2}$ hours, basting immediately and twice more during cooking.
2. Meanwhile, blanch the shredded cabbage for 2 minutes in boiling water, then drain and set aside.
3. Melt the butter in a flameproof casserole and cook the onion gently until soft. Remove the onion, mix it with the cabbage and add the sultanas. Season to taste.
4. Put the apples into the bottom of the casserole in which the onion cooked; put the cabbage mixture on top and press down well.
5. Cover closely with foil and then with the lid of the casserole and cook very gently on top of the cooker for 15 minutes then transfer the cabbage cake to the oven, with the pork, for 40 minutes.
6. To serve, put the pork on a warm dish and keep hot. Discard most of the fat from the roasting tin and stir 1 tablespoon flour into the remainder. Stir in the stock, boil for 2 minutes, season to taste and serve in a gravy boat.
7. Turn out the cabbage cake on to a hot dish by running a knife round the sides of the casserole and turning upside down. Sprinkle with parsley and arrange the egg like a flower on the top.

RABBIT AND ONION PIE

This traditional Welsh country recipe can also be adapted for chicken. Use 6 breasts of chicken portions instead of the rabbit and proceed in exactly the same way.

Serves 4–6
50 g (2 oz) cooking fat
1 rabbit, about 750 g (1½ lb), jointed, or 6 joints
225 g (8 oz) ham or bacon, thinly sliced
3 medium onions, peeled and finely sliced
salt
pepper
600 ml (1 pint) stock (can be made with stock cube)
1 sprig thyme
1 bay leaf
Flaky pastry:
225 g (8 oz) self-raising flour
¼ teaspoon salt
175 g (6 oz) butter or margarine
1 teaspoon lemon juice
150 ml (¼ pint) iced or very cold water
1 egg, beaten

Preparation time: 25 minutes, plus cooling
Cooking time: 1 hour 45 minutes
Oven: 200°C, 400°F, Gas Mark 6;
then: 180°C, 350°F, Gas Mark 4

1. Melt the fat in a large saucepan, add the rabbit, bacon and onions and fry for 5 minutes.
2. Season with salt and pepper, add the stock and herbs and simmer gently for 1 hour (30 minutes for chicken). Remove from the heat and cool.
3. Sieve the flour and salt into a bowl. Rub into it 25 g (1 oz) of the butter and add the lemon juice. Add the water slowly, stirring all the time until a smooth paste is formed.
4. Roll the dough out lightly on a floured board, then dab it with small pieces of butter, using a knife blade. Sprinkle with a pinch of flour. Fold the pastry towards you and pinch the edges so that it forms an envelope. Roll as before, rolling away from the joined edge and towards the fold so that the air is not forced out. Dab with butter again, sprinkle with flour, fold towards you, and roll once more. Repeat until all the butter has been used and you have an oblong shape about 1 cm (½ inch) thick.
5. Roll out to 3 mm (⅛ inch) thick and a little larger than the pie dish to be used.
6. Fill the pie dish with the cold rabbit mixture and cover with the pastry, knocking back the edges and pressing down firmly. Make a vent to let the steam escape. Roll out the pastry trimmings and cut out decorative leaves for the top, if liked. Brush the pastry with the beaten egg and bake in a preheated oven for 25 minutes. Lower the temperature, cover the pastry with foil and cook for a further 15 minutes.

From the top, anti-clockwise: *Rabbit and onion pie, Boiled leg of lamb with caper sauce, Loin of pork with cabbage cake from the Welsh Marches*

FRUIT CAKE FROM LLANDUDNO

This rich fruit cake was made for special occasions and sometimes iced instead of decorated with almonds.

Makes a 23 cm (9 inch) cake
225 g (8 oz) butter
100 g (4 oz) caster sugar
4 eggs, separated
1 teaspoon grated orange rind
1 teaspoon ground cinnamon
100 g (4 oz) ground almonds
50 g (2 oz) ground rice
350 g (12 oz) self-raising flour
225 g (8 oz) raisins, finely chopped
100 g (4 oz) currants, finely chopped
50 g (2 oz) glacé cherries, finely chopped
100 g (4 oz) sultanas, finely chopped
To decorate:
25 g (1 oz) whole, blanched almonds or white icing

Preparation time: 10–15 minutes
Cooking time: 2½ hours
Oven: 180°C, 350°F, Gas Mark 4;
then: 150°C, 300°F, Gas Mark 2

1. Cream together the butter and sugar very thoroughly, then beat in the egg yolks, the orange rind and the cinnamon.
2. Mix the ground almonds and the ground rice into the flour and then add this, a little at a time, to the mixture, alternating with handfuls of the fruit. Beat well after each addition.
3. Whip the egg whites very stiffly and fold gently into the mixture.
4. Pour the mixture at once into a well-greased 23 cm (9 inch) cake tin, lined with greaseproof paper, and put in a preheated oven for half an hour.
5. Reduce the oven heat and cook for a further 2 hours. Half an hour before it should be cooked, open the oven and, without taking the cake out, quickly sprinkle the almonds or white icing over the top.
6. Cool in the tin on a wire tray then turn out and leave until cold.

WELSH CAKES

Slightly different from all other girdle (or griddle) cakes and scones because they are a little firmer, these are always known as 'Welsh cakes' whether they are served in Wales or anywhere else. They were originally served to cold, tired and hungry travellers, on their arrival at an inn, while waiting for supper.

Makes 12–15 cakes
225 g (8 oz) self-raising flour
salt
50 g (2 oz) butter
50 g (2 oz) margarine
75 g (3 oz) sugar
50 g (2 oz) currants or sultanas
1 egg
milk if required
To serve:
sugar and butter

Preparation time: 5 minutes
Cooking time: 5 minutes

1. Sift together the flour and salt and rub in the butter and margarine.
2. Stir in the sugar and the fruit. Whisk the egg and add to the mixture. Then knead the whole to a firm dough, using a little milk if necessary.
3. Roll out to 5 mm (¼ inch) thickness and cut in 7.5 cm (3 inch) circles.
4. Slip on to a hot griddle or put in a preheated heavy frying pan and cook on each side, turning once, until a light golden brown.
5. Sprinkle each cake with sugar and put a dab of butter on each. Serve on a hot dish.

BRECON LIGHT CAKES

Makes 16 cakes
2 eggs
2 tablespoons orange juice
100 g (4 oz) self-raising flour
¼ teaspoon salt
50 g (2 oz) caster sugar
2–3 tablespoons milk
25 g (1 oz) margarine for frying
25 g (1 oz) soft brown sugar

Preparation time: 5 minutes
Cooking time: 5–10 minutes, according to size of frying pan

1. Beat the eggs together with half the orange juice.
2. Sift the flour and salt into a bowl and stir in the caster sugar.
3. Add the egg mixture, stirring well, and then beat in enough milk to make a fairly thin batter.
4. Melt the margarine in a heavy frying pan and, when it is just beginning to sizzle, drop in single tablespoons of the mixture, well separated, allowing them to spread to make 5–7 cm (2–3 inch) rounds. Cook until golden brown and then turn to cook the other side.
5. Drain briefly on absorbent kitchen paper. Place on a serving dish, sprinkle over the remaining orange juice and the brown sugar.

From the top, clockwise: *Fruit cake from Llandudno, Brecon light cakes, Stone cream, Welsh cakes*

STONE CREAM

This particular recipe came from a Welsh family, but it is a traditional cold sweet. It can be made with chopped strawberries or raspberries under the cream, but they are not really as good as the winter version with apricot jam.

Serves 6
225 g (8 oz) apricot jam
1 tablespoon brandy
1 tablespoon lemon juice
1 teaspoon grated lemon rind
15 g ($\frac{1}{2}$ oz) gelatine
2 tablespoons warm water
600 ml (1 pint) single cream
50 g (2 oz) icing sugar

Preparation time: 25 minutes plus chilling
Cooking time: 5 minutes

1. Mix the jam, brandy, lemon juice and rind together and spread over the bottom of a glass serving bowl or 6 individual glass dishes.
2. Stir the gelatine in the warm water until it is swelled and quite soft.
3. Put the cream in a heavy pan and bring just to boiling point, stirring in the icing sugar as it heats. When it is just boiling, add the gelatine and stir well. Allow to cool and when nearly cold stir well and pour over the jam mixture.
4. Chill for at least an hour before serving. Stone cream can be decorated with glacé cherries and angelica, but is traditionally served plain.

 The MIDLANDS

Cheshire, Derbyshire, Nottinghamshire, Staffordshire, Shropshire, Oxfordshire, Gloucestershire, Leicestershire, Warwickshire, Hereford and Worcester, Northamptonshire and Bedfordshire.

The Midlands, once described as 'the wide girdle of England in which she carries her industrial wealth', was the centre of the Industrial Revolution. However, it also included some of the most valuable agricultural land in the country, which is still thriving today. Midland cheeses, for example, such as Leicester and Double Gloucester, were, and are, famous; beef cattle fattened easily on the rich pastures and sheep flourished and produced the best wool in England on the Cotswold Hills. Indeed, the early breed, which was very hardy and very large and had long, crinkled fleeces, were known affectionately as Cotswold Lions. They were also considered excellent to eat.

The beautiful Vale of Evesham in Worcestershire, protected by the surrounding hills, is one of the greatest fruit-growing areas of England, and is renowned for apples and plums.

Although there was much good farming and fruit growing which abundantly supplied the markets of the industrial towns, people of the Midlands retained their taste for game.

The part of the Midlands called the Shires (Leicestershire, Rutland and Northamptonshire) formed the greatest hunting country in England and this led to a desire for substantial dishes on hunting days. In the nineteenth and early twentieth centuries, boiled eggs and Melton Mowbray pie often formed part of the high tea served to those who returned from hunting, to be followed by dinner some three hours later.

Hare was much sought after and venison was poached in Sherwood Forest or sometimes legitimately hunted and sold in Nottingham. Men who lived near Wychwood Forest and the nearby wooded country were accounted great poachers and could always sell any surplus venison or game birds direct to Oxford Colleges, where it was served at the High Tables at College Feasts.

Pies were a speciality. Melton Mowbray Pie, for which a traditional recipe is given in this book, is reckoned to be the best pork pie in the world. In Medieval times, the City of Gloucester was required every year to send to London a pie of lampreys, caught in the Severn, as part of its dues to the Crown.

Ironbridge, Shropshire

SUMMER SOUP

This soup comes from a great house in Shropshire. The delicious delicate flavour depends on all the vegetables and herbs being fresh from the garden.

1 lettuce, washed and cut into 1 cm (½ inch) strips
100 g (4 oz) fresh spinach, chopped
½ cucumber, peeled and cut into 1 cm (½ inch) cubes
2 medium onions, peeled and chopped
225 g (8 oz) potatoes, peeled and cut into 1 cm (½ inch) cubes
1 litre (1¾ pints) chicken stock
12 parsley sprigs
2 bay leaves
6 thyme sprigs
3 lemon thyme sprigs
½ teaspoon salt
½ teaspoon white pepper
300 ml (½ pint) double cream
To garnish:
1 tablespoon finely chopped mint and parsley mixed

Preparation time: 30 minutes plus chilling
Cooking time: 30 minutes

1. Place all the vegetables in a large saucepan with the stock. Tie the herbs in a bunch and add to the pan with the salt and pepper.
2. Bring to the boil and simmer, covered, for 30 minutes.
3. Remove from the heat, discard the herbs and allow the soup to cool completely.
4. When the soup is cold, stir in all but 1 tablespoon of the cream and chill in the refrigerator for at least 1 hour before serving.
5. Ladle the chilled soup into 4 bowls. Swirl a teaspoon of cream on top of each and sprinkle with the chopped mint and parsley.

CHESTER POTTED MEAT

Potted meats are the English equivalents of the pâtés and terrines of France.

Serves 8
1 kg (2 lb) boneless pork, skin removed
225 g (8 oz) cooked ham
225 g (8 oz) pig's liver
2 garlic cloves, crushed (optional)
½ teaspoon ground mace
1 teaspoon salt
½ teaspoon coarsely ground black pepper
85 ml (3 fl oz) brandy
6 rashers streaky bacon, rinded
2 bay leaves

Preparation time: 25 minutes plus cooling, then chilling overnight
Cooking time: 2 hours
Oven: 180°C, 350°F, Gas Mark 4

1. Put the pork, including the fat, through a mincer or food processor, and do the same with the ham and liver.
2. Mix the minced meats with the garlic, stirring well, and season with the mace, salt and pepper. Add the brandy and stir well again.
3. Line a 1.25 kg (3 lb) earthenware terrine dish or loaf tin with the bacon rashers and lay the bay leaves in the bottom. Then put in the prepared meat mixture, pressing it well down with a wooden spoon.
4. Cover tightly with foil and stand in a roasting tin. Pour in boiling water to come about 2 cm (¾ inch) up the sides. Bake in a preheated oven for 2 hours, or until a skewer comes out clean when inserted into the centre. Add more boiling water to the tin if necessary.
5. Remove from the oven and allow to cool, then weight down and chill in the refrigerator overnight. Turn out on to a serving plate and cut into 1 cm (½ inch) slices to serve.

THREE-FRUIT SAVOURY COCKTAIL

Serves 6
1 small melon
2 large avocados
¼ teaspoon salt
1 tablespoon lemon juice
1 teaspoon caster sugar
450 g (1 lb) tomatoes, skinned, quartered and seeded
Dressing:
4 tablespoons olive oil
2 tablespoons wine vinegar
1 teaspoon salt
1 teaspoon caster sugar
½ teaspoon mustard powder

Preparation time: 20 minutes plus chilling

1. Cut the melon in half and remove the seeds. Scoop out the flesh with a melon baller or cut it into neat cubes with a knife.
2. Stone and peel the avocados, cut the flesh in quarters lengthways and cut each piece into quarters crossways.
3. Sprinkle the avocados lightly with salt and lemon juice and place in 6 individual glass dishes. Sprinkle salt and sugar on the tomatoes and place on top of the avocados. Add the melon and chill for at least 1 hour or overnight.
4. Just before serving, thoroughly combine the dressing ingredients and spoon over the salads.

HADDOCK AND BACON POT PIE

Serves 2–3
450 g (1 lb) smoked haddock fillets
½ teaspoon freshly ground black pepper
4 rashers back bacon, rinded and diced
40 g (1½ oz) butter
350 g (12 oz) tomatoes, skinned, quartered and seeded
75 g (3 oz) fine fresh white breadcrumbs

Preparation time: 20 minutes
Cooking time: 40 minutes
Oven: 180°C, 350°F, Gas Mark 4

1. Place the haddock fillets in a large frying pan, pour in boiling water just to cover and poach gently for 10 minutes. Remove from the heat and cool slightly, then flake, removing skin and any bones. Season with the pepper.
2. Fry the bacon without added fat, until softened.
3. Grease a baking dish with one-third of the butter. Place the fish in the dish, then the tomatoes and the bacon. Sprinkle with the breadcrumbs and dot with the remaining butter.
4. Bake in a preheated oven for 30 minutes, until the topping is crisp and golden brown.

CURRIED PRAWNS

½ teaspoon chilli powder
½ teaspoon ground turmeric
¼ teaspoon ground mace
¼ teaspoon freshly ground black pepper
¼ teaspoon ground ginger
2 tablespoons vegetable oil
450 g (1 lb) frozen peeled prawns, defrosted and well drained
3 tablespoons double cream
4 slices white bread

Preparation time: 10 minutes
Cooking time: 10 minutes

1. Heat a small frying pan. Mix together all the spices and tip them into it. Holding the pan just above the heat, work the spices together with a wooden spoon.
2. Stir the oil into the hot dry spices and work them together over the heat.
3. Add the prawns and stir for 1 minute, until thoroughly coated. Stir in the cream and cook for 1 further minute, stirring well.
4. Turn the prawn mixture into 4 individual heated gratin dishes and keep hot. Toast the bread, remove the crusts and cut each slice diagonally into 4 triangles.
5. To serve, garnish each dish with toast triangles.

FISH PIE

Fish pie is made all over the country, but this one, from Leicester, differs from the more usual recipes in which the fish is flaked in the sauce.

1 kg (2 lb) potatoes, peeled and cut into chunks
750 g (1½ lb) cod, hake or haddock fillets, skinned and cut into 4 equal pieces
salt
pepper
900 ml (1½ pints) milk
75 g (3 oz) butter
40 g (1½ oz) plain flour

Preparation time: 15 minutes plus cooling
Cooking time: 50 minutes
Oven: 180°C, 350°F, Gas Mark 4

1. Boil the potatoes in a large saucepan of salted water until tender (15–20 minutes).
2. Meanwhile, grease a wide, shallow ovenproof dish and lay the pieces of fish in two layers in it. Season with salt and pepper and pour over 750 ml (1¼ pints) of the milk. Closely cover with foil and bake in a preheated oven for 25 minutes.
3. Drain the potatoes and pass them through a mouli-légumes or sieve. Add 40 g (1½ oz) butter and 150 ml (¼ pint) milk and beat until soft and creamy. Set aside to cool, but do not chill.

4. Just before removing the fish from the oven, melt 25 g (1 oz) of the butter in a medium saucepan, sprinkle in the flour and cook, stirring, for 1–2 minutes. Remove from the heat. Strain the cooking liquid from the fish and gradually stir into the butter and flour mixture. Return to the heat and cook, stirring, for 2–3 minutes. Season to taste.
5. Pour the sauce evenly over the fish, and leave to cool completely.
6. Spoon the potato over the fish and lightly smooth the surface, then mark the top in a pattern with the fork. Dot with the remaining butter.
7. Bake near the top of the preheated oven for about 25 minutes, until the fish is heated through and the topping is browned.

Variation: For a richer dish, stir 85 ml (3 fl oz) white wine into the roux before adding the milk and 2 tablespoons of double cream into the sauce just before pouring it over the fish.

From the left: *Haddock and bacon pot pie, Curried prawns, Fish pie*

JUGGED HARE

❦

This is a dish which goes back to the Middle Ages and probably to Roman times. Originally, the joints and saddle of hare were fitted into an earthenware jug with the stock and wine and the jug stood, covered, in a cauldron of boiling water over an open fire. Nowadays, the pieces are usually cooked in a deep casserole, standing in a roasting tin of water in the oven, though if you have a casserole which will stand in a very large saucepan or preserving pan, the dish can be cooked on top of the stove if you prefer. The blood of the hare used to be saved and added to the gravy after it had boiled and cooled a little (as blood curdles if boiled) but most people prefer to omit this today.

Serves 6
100 g (4 oz) fine oatmeal
salt
white pepper
1 hare, cleaned, skinned and jointed
75 g (3 oz) butter
1 medium onion, peeled and stuck with cloves
1 large cooking apple, peeled, cored and sliced
1 small lemon, sliced
225 g (8 oz) mushrooms, sliced
1 sprig each thyme, parsley, marjoram, tied in a
bunch or 1 bouquet garni
3 bay leaves
120 ml (4 fl oz) red wine
600 ml (1 pint) beef stock
12 forcemeat balls (page 20)

Preparation time: 40 minutes
Cooking time: 3 hours
Oven: 180°C, 350°F, Gas Mark 4

---

1. Season half the oatmeal with ½ teaspoon salt and ½ teaspoon pepper and rub it over the hare joints. Heat 50 g (2 oz) of the butter in a large frying pan, add the hare and fry quickly, turning, to seal and brown on all sides. Remove from the heat.
2. Place the head, neck and ribs of the hare (which will not be served, as there is little meat on them, but which will enrich the gravy) in the bottom of a large casserole. Sprinkle with half the remaining oatmeal.
3. Pack in the hare joints and then the onion, apple, lemon, mushrooms and herbs. Sprinkle with the remaining oatmeal and season. Combine the wine and stock and pour into the casserole.
4. Cover tightly and stand in a roasting tin. Pour in boiling water to come halfway up the sides of the casserole and cook in a preheated oven for 3 hours.
5. Towards the end of the cooking time fry the forcemeat balls in the remaining butter.
6. Transfer the hare joints to a serving dish and

strain the gravy, discarding the head, neck and ribs. Taste and adjust the seasoning, if necessary. Pour the gravy over the hare. Arrange the forcemeat balls around the edge of the dish and serve very hot.

PIGEONS IN PASTRY

❦

Pigeons are very good cooked in pastry and make an impressive dish for a dinner party. Quails can be cooked in the same way, allowing 2 per person.

Serves 6
750 g (1½ lb) Flaky pastry (page 61)
100 g (4 oz) butter
6 young pigeons, cleaned and trussed
100 g (4 oz) mushrooms, sliced
1 teaspoon chopped thyme or ½ teaspoon dried thyme
salt
freshly ground black pepper
3 tablespoons red wine or 2 tablespoons sherry
600 ml (1 pint) well-seasoned, thickened brown
gravy
1 egg, well beaten

Preparation time: 30 minutes
Cooking time: 55 minutes
Oven: 230°C, 450°F, Gas Mark 8
then: 180°C, 350°F, Gas Mark 4

---

1. Roll out the pastry to about 5 mm (¼ inch) thickness and leave to rest in a cool place.
2. Heat the butter in a large frying pan, add the pigeons and fry, turning, to brown on all sides. Remove from the pan and set aside while lightly frying the mushrooms in the same butter.
3. Roll the pastry out again, a little thinner than before, and cut out 6 circles, each large enough to cover a pigeon completely.
4. Place a pigeon in the centre of each pastry circle, top with a few mushroom slices and sprinkle with the thyme, salt and pepper. Mix the wine with the gravy and pour a spoonful over each pigeon.
5. Lift the pastry up round each pigeon and pinch well together at the top to seal. Brush all over with the beaten egg.
6. Bake near the top of a preheated oven for 10 minutes, then move the pigeon parcels to the lower part of the oven, place a sheet of foil lightly over them and reduce the heat. Bake for a further 35 minutes. Meanwhile reheat the remaining gravy.
7. Transfer the pigeon parcels very carefully to a heated flat serving dish and serve immediately, with the gravy handed separately in a jug.

From the bottom:
Pigeons in pastry with
gravy, Jugged hare

LAMB CHOPS WITH CHESTNUTS

❦

This is a recipe from Warwick. Many people only ever serve chestnuts with the turkey at Christmas. This is a pity, as they are particularly good with lamb and pork, and add interest to a simple dish of chops.

4 lamb loin chops, trimmed
2 tablespoons plain flour
50 g (2 oz) butter
2 large onions, peeled and finely sliced
750 g (1½ lb) chestnuts, peeled, skinned and boiled until just tender
450 ml (¾ pint) beef stock
300 ml (½ pint) red wine
¼ teaspoon ground mace
½ teaspoon dried thyme
½ teaspoon salt
¼ teaspoon freshly ground black pepper

Preparation time: 40 minutes
Cooking time: 2¼ hours
Oven: 150°C, 300°F, Gas Mark 2

1. Sprinkle the chops with the flour. Heat the butter in a large frying pan, add the chops and fry briskly for 2 minutes on each side.
2. Transfer the chops to a fairly deep casserole. Fry the onions in the same butter for about 5 minutes, until soft and transparent, then scatter over the chops. Add the chestnuts.
3. Mix together the stock, wine, mace, thyme, salt and pepper and pour over the chops. Cover and cook in a preheated oven for 2 hours, or until the chops are tender and cooked through. Serve with plain boiled potatoes and a dish of baked red or white cabbage.

FRICASSEE OF PORK WITH APPLE RINGS

❦

750 g (1½ lb) pork fillet, trimmed
3 tablespoons plain flour
salt
freshly ground black pepper
50 g (2 oz) butter
1 large onion, peeled and thinly sliced
300 ml (½ pint) hot chicken stock
300 ml (½ pint) milk
1 bay leaf
1 sprig each thyme, parsley, marjoram or 1 bouquet garni
Apple rings:
25 g (1 oz) butter
2 dessert apples, peeled, cored and cut across in 5 mm (¼ inch) rings

Preparation time: 20 minutes
Cooking time: 45 minutes

1. Cut the pork into neat pieces about 5 × 2.5 cm (2 × 1 inch) and 5 mm (¼ inch) thick. Season 2 tablespoons of the flour with ¼ teaspoon each of salt and pepper and place in a polythene bag. Add the pork and shake until thoroughly coated.

2. Melt half the butter in a flameproof casserole, add the onion and fry gently for about 5 minutes till soft but not coloured. Transfer to a plate and set aside.

3. In the same pan fry the pork, adding a little more butter if necessary, for 2 minutes on each side, until lightly browned. Transfer to the plate with the onion.

4. Stir the remaining flour into the casserole, scraping down the sides with a wooden spoon. Cook for 1–2 minutes. Gradually stir in the chicken stock and finally stir in the milk. Cook for 2–3 minutes, stirring, until thickened and smooth.

5. Stir the herbs into the sauce and then put in the pork and the onions. Cover and simmer very gently for 30 minutes, until the pork is tender.

6. Meanwhile, melt 25 g (1 oz) butter in a frying pan, add the apple rings and fry gently for 2 or 3 minutes on each side.

7. Remove the herbs from the casserole, taste and adjust the seasoning, if necessary, arrange the apple rings round the edge of the casserole and serve.

From the left: *Lamb chops with chestnuts, Fricassée of pork with apple rings*

POT ROASTED BEEF

4 tablespoons vegetable oil
25 g (1 oz) butter
1.25–1.5 kg (2½–3 lb) topside or silverside of beef
2 large onions, peeled and quartered
2 large carrots, scraped and cut into
1 cm (½ inch) slices
1 bouquet garni or 2 sprigs each thyme, parsley and marjoram
4 black peppercorns
½ teaspoon salt
150 ml (¼ pint) red wine mixed with 450 ml (¾ pint) water
2 teaspoons cornflour

Preparation time: 30 minutes
Cooking time: 3 hours 20 minutes
Oven: 150°C, 300°F, Gas Mark 2

1. Heat the oil and butter in a flameproof casserole, add the beef and turn until browned.
2. Reduce the heat and pack the vegetables all round the beef. Add the herbs, peppercorns and salt. Pour in the wine and water.
3. Closely cover the casserole with foil and then its lid and cook in a preheated oven for 3 hours, until the beef is tender and cooked through.
4. Transfer the beef to a heated serving dish. Discard the herbs. Lift out the vegetables with a perforated spoon and place round the beef. Keep hot while making the sauce.
5. Bring the cooking liquid in the casserole to the boil. Mix the cornflour with a little water to make a smooth paste, pour a little of the boiling gravy on to it, stirring well, and pour back into the boiling gravy in the casserole, stirring constantly. If the sauce is too thick, thin with a little stock or water and return to the boil. Pour the sauce over the beef and vegetables and serve.

BRUSSELS SPROUTS AU GRATIN

450 g (1 lb) Brussels sprouts, fresh or frozen
salt
3 rashers streaky bacon, rinded and diced
50 g (2 oz) Cheddar cheese, grated
25 g (1 oz) fine fresh white breadcrumbs

Preparation time: 10 minutes
Cooking time: 20 minutes

1. Cook the sprouts in boiling salted water until they are just tender. Drain well.
2. Meanwhile, fry the bacon without added fat until crisp. Drain and keep hot.

3. Add the sprouts to the bacon fat in the pan and toss for 2–3 minutes over moderate heat. Lift out with a perforated spoon and mix with the chopped bacon in a flameproof dish.
4. Sprinkle the top with the cheese and crumbs and set under a preheated hot grill until browned.

BEDFORDSHIRE CLANGERS

This very old recipe has always been known as Bedfordshire Clangers although only one large roll was made at a time.

Serves 6
450 g (1 lb) chuck steak or lean pork, all skin and fat removed and cut into 1 cm (½ inch) dice
100 g (4 oz) ox kidney or 1 pig's kidney, skinned, cored and cut into 5 mm (¼ inch) dice
1 large onion, peeled and very finely chopped
75 g (3 oz) seedless raisins
2 large cooking apples, peeled, cored and cut into 1 cm (½ inch) dice
salt
pepper .
Suet crust:
225 g (8 oz) shredded suet
1 teaspoon salt
450 g (1 lb) self-raising flour, sifted
150 ml (¼ pint) cold water

Preparation time: 40 minutes
Cooking time: 3 hours 40 minutes
Oven: 180°C, 350°F, Gas Mark 4

1. Season the meat well and mix with the onion.
2. To make the suet crust, add the suet and salt to the flour in a mixing bowl and mix lightly together. Pour in the water and stir to mix, adding a little more water if necessary, to make a firm dough. Sift over a little flour and roll out on a lightly floured surface to a large rectangle, 5 mm (¼ inch) thick. Cut in half lengthways.
3. Sprinkle the raisins on one piece of dough and sprinkle the apple dice on top. Lay the second piece of dough on top, to form a sandwich. Sprinkle with a little flour and gently roll out, so that the apple and raisins are embedded in the crust.
4. Spread the seasoned meat and onion over the dough, leaving a 2½ cm (1 inch) border round the edges. Dampen the edges with milk and then roll up tightly, press the ends well together.
5. Wrap the suet roll in buttered foil and then tie it in a cloth dusted with flour on the inside.
6. Place in a large saucepan or fish kettle, cover with boiling water and boil for 3½ hours.
7. Lift out the roll and allow to cool slightly, then unwrap and place on a flat serving dish in the preheated oven for 10 minutes. Serve cut into slices, with gravy or tomato sauce.

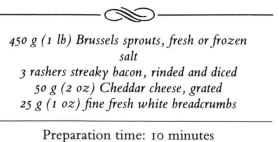

From the top: Brussels sprouts au gratin, Pot roasted beef

MELTON MOWBRAY PIE

Pies of this type, intended to be eaten cold,
were made as far back as the Middle Ages.

Serves 6
450 g (1 lb) pork bones
2 medium onions, peeled and quartered
2 sage leaves
1 bay leaf
2 sprigs marjoram
salt
freshly ground black pepper
1 kg (2 lb) leg or shoulder of pork, trimmed, and cut
into 5 mm (¼ inch) dice
25 g (1 oz) butter
Crust:
450 g (1 lb) plain flour
100 g (4 oz) butter
100 g (4 oz) lard
150 ml (¼ pint) milk and water mixed
1 egg, well beaten

Preparation time: 40 minutes
Cooking time: 4 hours
Oven: 190°C, 375°F, Gas Mark 5
then: 160°C, 325°F, Gas Mark 3

1. Place the pork bones in a large saucepan with
the onions, 1 sage leaf, the bay leaf, marjoram,
salt and pepper. Pour in 900 ml (1½ pints) boiling
water. Boil for 2 hours, to reduce the stock to 600
ml (1 pint) of liquid, then cool and skim off all fat.
Remove and discard the bones and check seasoning. The stock will jell as it cools. **A**
2. Mix together the diced pork, 1 teaspoon salt, ½
teaspoon pepper and the remaining sage leaf,
finely chopped.
3. To make the crust, sift the flour with ½
teaspoon salt. Add 50 g (2 oz) of the fat and rub in
with the fingertips until the mixture resembles
fine breadcrumbs.
4. Place the remaining fat in a saucepan with the
milk and water and bring to the boil. Make a well
in the flour and, when the liquid is boiling,
gradually pour it in, stirring with a wooden spoon

until it is all absorbed. Knead well and let the pastry stand for 10 minutes.

5. Roll out the pastry to a large circle 1–2 cm (½–¾ inch) thick. Stand a 17.5 cm (7 inch) deep cake tin, open end up, in the centre of the pastry circle and work it up to cover the sides. Trim the top of the pie with a sharp knife. Turn the pastry-covered tin on its side and roll it a few times to smooth the outside and loosen the tin. Gently stand it up again and work the tin out; the pastry case will remain standing.

6. Pack the pork mixture closely into the case to within 5 mm (¼ inch) of the top. Spoon in 2 tablespoons of the jellied stock and dot the top of the meat with the butter.

7. Roll out all the pastry trimmings and cut out a lid that is larger than the top of the pie case. Brush the top edges of the pie case with a little milk, press on the lid and firmly crimp the edges all round to make a raised ridge. Make a small hole in the centre of the lid and roll out any pastry trimmings to make leaves to decorate the top of the pie.

8. Brush the pie all over with half the beaten egg. Bake in the centre of the preheated oven for 20 minutes to set the pastry; then reduce the temperature and cover the top of the pie with aluminium foil. Bake in the lower part of the oven for a further 1¾ hours.

9. Remove the pie from the oven about 10 minutes before the end of the baking time and brush over again with the remaining beaten egg. Return to the oven to finish baking.

10. Reheat the jellied stock until it is liquid. As soon as the baked pie is removed from the oven, carefully pour the stock through the hole in the top, until the pie is full. Cool, then leave in the refrigerator to become quite cool and allow the stock to set.

A The jellied stock may be made beforehand. It will keep in the refrigerator for 24 hours or it can, of course, be frozen.

Melton Mowbray pie

HUNTSMAN'S OMELETTE

This recipe comes from Gloucester. It is very savoury and filling and is an egg dish, rather than a true omelette.

100 g (4 oz) fine fresh white breadcrumbs
salt
freshly ground black pepper
freshly grated nutmeg
85 ml (3 fl oz) double cream
120 g (4½ oz) butter
1 medium onion, peeled and finely chopped
50 g (2 oz) mushrooms, sliced
1 chicken liver or 50 g (2 oz) lamb's or pig's liver, trimmed and finely chopped
2 lamb's kidneys or 1 pig's kidney, skinned, cored and finely chopped
8 eggs

Preparation time: 40 minutes
Cooking time: 15 minutes

1. Place the breadcrumbs in a bowl and season with salt, pepper and nutmeg. Pour in the cream, stir and leave for 30 minutes for the crumbs to swell.
2. Meanwhile, heat 50 g (2 oz) of the butter in a frying pan, add the onion and mushrooms and fry gently, turning, until just soft. Push them to the side of the pan and fry the liver and kidneys for 4 minutes, turning constantly. Mix the mushrooms and onions with the liver and kidneys and place in a small dish to keep warm.
3. Beat the eggs well with ½ teaspoon salt, then beat in the breadcrumb mixture.
4. Melt a further 50 g (2 oz) of the butter in a large frying pan. As soon as it begins to foam, pour in the egg mixture and cook for 2 minutes, drawing the sides into the middle with a palette knife. Put the meat mixture into the unset centre of the eggs and dot with the remaining butter.
5. Set the pan under a preheated grill for 1 minute, until the egg puffs up. Divide into quarters in the pan and serve immediately.

BAKED WINTER CABBAGE WITH APPLES AND SULTANAS

This way of cooking winter cabbage improves its flavour and is particularly good with a pork or ham dish.

Serves 6
1 kg (2 lb) hard white or red cabbage, outer leaves and stalk removed, very finely sliced
¼ teaspoon ground mace
¼ teaspoon ground turmeric
100 g (4 oz) sultanas
2 dessert apples, peeled, cored and cut into eighths
1 teaspoon salt
½ teaspoon freshly ground black pepper
50 g (2 oz) butter
150 ml (¼ pint) cold water

Preparation time: 10 minutes
Cooking time: 1½ hours or 2 hours
Oven: 180°C, 350°F, Gas Mark 4

1. Mix the cabbage with the spices, sultanas and apple slices. Season with the salt and pepper.
2. Butter a deep casserole with half the butter and put in the cabbage mixture. Stir in water. Dot the top with the remaining butter, cover closely with foil and then the lid of the casserole.
3. Bake in the preheated oven until tender (1½ hours for white cabbage, 2 hours for red cabbage).

PORT WINE JELLY

This recipe, from Birmingham, makes a superb and unexpected dinner party sweet. It is rather expensive but well worth it.

Serves 6–8
50 g (2 oz) powdered gelatine
8 tablespoons water
600 ml (1 pint) port wine
75 g (3 oz) caster sugar
300 ml (½ pint) red wine
450 g (1 lb) blackcurrant jam
¼ teaspoon ground cinnamon
¼ teaspoon freshly ground nutmeg
3 teaspoons lemon juice
150 ml (¼ pint) water
300 ml (½ pint) whipping cream, whipped

Preparation time: 15 minutes plus setting
Cooking time: 25 minutes

1. Soak the gelatine in 2 tablespoons water for a few minutes, until spongy. Mix with the rest of the water, half the port and all the remaining ingredients, except the cream, in a saucepan and stir over a low heat until just below boiling point. Remove from the heat, add the remaining port and stir well.
2. Rinse a 1.2 litre (2 pint) jelly mould with cold water and strain the port mixture into it. Chill in the refrigerator for at least 6 hours, until set.
3. Turn the jelly out on to a serving dish and pipe the cream round the sides. Serve immediately.

From the top, clockwise: *Port wine jelly, Baked winter cabbage with apples and sultanas, Huntsman's omelette*

SAND CAKE

Once more frequently made than nowadays. However, a recipe from Leicester produces a very unusual and delicious cake. The use of cornflour makes it very light and smooth in texture.

75 g (3 oz) butter or margarine
100 g (4 oz) caster sugar
2 eggs, well beaten
finely grated rind of 1 lemon
100 g (4 oz) cornflour
25 g (1 oz) plain flour
1½ teaspoons baking powder
Icing:
3 teaspoons lemon juice
1 teaspoon water
100 g (4 oz) icing sugar, sifted

Preparation time: 20 minutes
Cooking time: 55 minutes
Oven: 180°C, 350°F, Gas Mark 4

1. Cream the butter with the sugar, until light, fluffy and pale. Gradually beat in the eggs and add the lemon rind. Sift the cornflour with the flour and baking powder and fold into the mixture.
2. Turn into a well-greased 450 g (1 lb) loaf tin. Bake in the preheated oven for 50 minutes, until a skewer inserted into the centre comes out clean. Turn on to a wire rack and leave to cool.
3. To make the icing, mix the lemon juice and water into the icing sugar in a small saucepan. Stir over low heat until melted and just warm.
4. Immediately pour the icing over the cake and allow it to run down the sides. Leave to set.

ORANGE TART

Tradition has it that this recipe, from an eighteenth-century Oxford manuscript, was a favourite of George III's queen, Charlotte of Mecklenburg.

Serves 6
225 g (8 oz) shortcrust pastry
finely grated rind of 3 medium oranges
finely grated rind and juice of 1 lemon
400 ml (14 fl oz) orange juice
150 g (5 oz) caster sugar
3 tablespoons cornflour
5 eggs, separated

Preparation time: 30 minutes
Cooking time: 1 hour
Oven: 200°C, 400°F, Gas Mark 6; then 150°C, 300°F, Gas Mark 2

1. Roll out the pastry and use to line a 23 cm (9 inch) flan tin. Bake blind for 15 minutes, then remove the beans and paper and bake for a further 5 minutes.
2. Mix the orange and lemon rinds and orange juice with 100 g (4 oz) sugar and the cornflour in a saucepan. Blend well and bring to the boil, stirring all the time. Lower the heat and cook for 1 minute. Remove from the heat and stir in the egg yolks and lemon juice. Pour the filling into the pastry case.
3. Lower the oven temperature. Beat the egg whites with the remaining sugar until they form stiff peaks. Pile the meringue on top, to cover the filling completely. Return to the oven and bake for 30 minutes, or until the meringue is crisp and lightly browned.

TIPSY CAKE

Tipsy cakes were traditionally served at ball suppers. This eighteenth century recipe is very ornamental.

Serves 8
1 large sponge cake or 8 small ones
3 tablespoons apricot jam
350 ml (12 fl oz) sweet sherry or madeira or marsala
3 tablespoons orange juice, strained
75 g (3 oz) caster sugar
600 ml (1 pint) double cream
225 g (8 oz) blanched almonds, split and toasted

Preparation time: 45 minutes plus chilling overnight
Cooking time: 5 minutes
Oven: 180°C, 350°F, Gas Mark 4

1. Cut the cake into 8 sections and stick them back together with apricot jam, or stick the 8 small cakes together.
2. Cut out a well in the top of the cake, reserving the cut-out piece to put back later. Fill the well with wine and pour the remaining wine all over the cake.
3. Chill in the refrigerator overnight, spooning the wine over the cake from time to time. Replace the cut-out piece of cake next day.
4. Whip the orange juice, sugar and cream until soft peaks form and spoon over the cake. Arrange the almonds in a decorative pattern over the cake. Serve immediately.

From the bottom, clockwise: *Tipsy cake, Orange tart, Sand cake*

EAST ANGLIA

The Eastern Counties: Norfolk, Suffolk, Cambridgeshire, Essex, Lincolnshire

Over the centuries, royalty, on progress to or from London through the eastern counties, travelled slowly across the green fields outside the city, which gave place to the deep forest and rolling farmlands. The monarch's routes were arranged to provide stops at the great houses of nobles who deserved and could afford the honour of a royal visit. We can get some idea of what the region had to offer from the account of the visit in 1561 of Queen Elizabeth I to Ingatestone Hall in Essex, the home of her Secretary of State, Sir William Petre. Not only a large part of Sir William's great house but also his household accounts have been preserved and we can see the detailed expenditure on food alone required for the Queen's visit. She spent two nights at Ingatestone Hall in July and these two nights clearly required a great deal of preparation. Early in the month Sir William rode down from London. With him went Mr Wilcocks, his chief cook who brought spices, colouring, 'turnsole', which gave a violet colour to jellies, 'grains', which produced a bright red-gold leaf for decorating jellies, and the 'subtleties' which were modelled in marzipan.

Servants were sent to the fens to catch wildfowl. Tenants and friends sent a stag, caponets (young capons), two pigs, apples, two lambs, fish and dozens of oysters. Quails, egrets and many pigeons were also brought to the kitchens, as well as a salmon, a turkey cock and a dozen peachicks.

Saffron came direct from Saffron Walden near Cambridge, where the fields were planted with the crocus whose stamens yields the spice, highly prized both for its delicate flavour and for the golden colour it imparted.

Queen Elizabeth arrived at about noon on Saturday, 19 July. In those days Saturdays were fish days when only one main meal could be served, with no meat, game or poultry. For a royal visit on a 'fysshe day' only a sturgeon, a fish reserved for royalty in England, was adequate and Sir William Petre sent for one from London. The cost of the two or three days' royal visit, in food and drink alone, was about £135, the equivalent of about £5,000 today.

East Anglia and the eastern counties stretch from Greater London, whose suburbs cover the south and east of Essex, to the Wash on the north-west coast of Norfolk and includes Suffolk, Cambridgeshire and the fen district of Lincolnshire. There are special points of interest relating to the regional cooking of each of these counties, but as a whole this part of England has a distinct character and tradition of its own. In general, it is a low-lying region, with most of its immense marshes drained and turned into rich farmland. Suffolk has some of the best wheat-growing land in England, while it is considered that the best poultry in the country comes from Norfolk.

BARLEY CREAM SOUP

This is an eighteenth century Essex recipe which brings out the very subtle flavour of the barley.

Serves 6
100 g (4 oz) pearl barley
1 litre (1¾ pints) chicken stock (cube will do)
150 ml (¼ pint) milk
150 ml (¼ pint) double cream
salt
pepper
25 g (1 oz) butter
2 teaspoons chopped parsley

Preparation time: 5 minutes
Cooking time: 2¼ hours

1. Blanch the barley for 1 minute in boiling water, then drain.
2. Add the drained barley to the chicken stock and simmer for 2 hours.
3. Pass through a fine mouli or liquidise. Add the milk, cream, salt and pepper and the butter cut into small pieces. Reheat and serve sprinkled with chopped parsley.

HUNTINGDON STUFFED PEARS

2 large, ripe pears
100 g (4 oz) Stilton cheese, firm but not hard
25 g (1 oz) soft butter
1 tablespoon double cream
freshly ground black pepper
25 g (1 oz) walnuts, finely chopped,
plus 4 walnut halves
4 crisp lettuce leaves
2 tablespoons lemon juice

Preparation time: 5 minutes

1. Peel, halve and core the pears, hollowing them out carefully.
2. Cream together the cheese, butter, cream, and black pepper, using either a blender or a bowl and wooden spoon. Add the chopped walnuts.
3. Fill the centres of the pears with the mixture and stand each on a lettuce leaf on small plates. Put a half-walnut in the centre of each.
4. Squeeze lemon juice over the unfilled parts of the pears to prevent them from discolouring.

STUFFED LETTUCE HEARTS

This recipe from an Essex manuscript makes a delicious starter and a change from the more traditional shrimps or prawns with lettuce.

175 g (6 oz) cooked pork, lamb or chicken, skinned
and chopped into 1 cm (½ inch) pieces
2 hardboiled eggs, peeled and finely chopped
¼ teaspoon ground mace
½ teaspoon salt
¼ teaspoon pepper
50 g (2 oz) butter, softened
1 tablespoon chopped parsley and chives mixed
½ cucumber, peeled and finely sliced
8 crisp heart leaves of lettuce
50 g (2 oz) walnuts, finely chopped

Preparation time: 20 minutes, plus chilling

1. Combine the meat, eggs, mace, salt and pepper and stir into the softened butter. Add the parsley and chives and mix well.
2. Arrange the cucumber slices on small plates. Divide the stuffing into 8 portions. Fill each lettuce leaf with a portion of stuffing and put 2 on each plate with the cucumber. Sprinkle with the walnuts.
3. Chill for not more than 2 hours and serve.

POTTED HAM

2 tablespoons vegetable oil
225 g (8 oz) onion, peeled and thinly sliced
450 g (1 lb) cooked ham
½ teaspoon cayenne pepper
15 g (½ oz) curry powder
1 teaspoon paprika
salt
150 ml (¼ pint) cider or red wine
50 g (2 oz) butter

Preparation time: 10 minutes
Cooking time: 30–40 minutes

1. Heat the oil in a frying pan and add the onions. Fry gently over low heat until tender, but not browned.
2. Finely mince the ham and onions together in a mincer or blender. Add the spices, mix well together and add salt to taste.
3. Put the cider in a saucepan, add the ham mixture and mix well. Simmer over low heat for 30 minutes, then remove from the heat and cool.
4. Pack in stone or pottery jars. Melt the butter in a saucepan over moderate heat. Skim off the foam and strain the yellow liquid into a bowl, leaving the milky residue in the pan. Pour the clarified butter on top of the jars to seal the ham. If the seal is unbroken it will keep for 2 months in the refrigerator.

From the top, clockwise: Potted ham, Barley cream soup, Huntingdon stuffed pears, Stuffed lettuce hearts

LOBSTER SALAD

Lobster is nowadays very expensive and its
delicious flavour is so delicate that it should
have no strong-tasting accompaniments. Crisp
lettuce sets it off best without other salad
vegetables. The mayonnaise should be a good
make or home-made and can have one
tablespoon double cream stirred into it, if it
seems too sharp-tasting.

1 large lobster, meat removed and coral and claws
saved or
2 small ones prepared in the same way
¼ teapsoon salt
freshly ground black pepper
150 ml (¼ pint) good mayonnaise
1 large crisp lettuce
4 tablespoons French dressing
3 hard-boiled eggs, cut in quarters longways
1 tablespoon finely chopped parsley

Preparation time: 30 minutes, plus chilling

1. Chop all the claw meat, season with salt and
pepper and reserve. Chop the rest of the lobster
meat and mix it with the coral and the
mayonnaise.
2. Remove the outer leaves and stems from the
lettuce and chop all but about a quarter.
3. Dress the chopped lettuce with French dressing
and pile in the centre of a flat serving dish. Pile the
lobster meat on top, arrange the remaining lettuce
leaves around the sides with the claw meat.
4. Arrange the egg quarters so that they resemble
flower petals. Garnish with the claws and sprinkle
parsley over all. Chill before serving.

POTTED SHRIMPS

Serves 6
450 g (1 lb) shelled shrimps or prawns
1 teaspoon ground mace
225 g (8 oz) butter
salt
¼ teaspoon cayenne pepper

Preparation time: 10 minutes, plus overnight
cooling
Cooking time: 10 minutes

1. Finely chop half the shellfish and mix the two
lots together with the mace.
2. Melt 175 g (6 oz) of the butter in a pan, but do
not let it boil. Stir in the shellfish and then add salt
and cayenne pepper to taste. Stir over low heat
until all the butter is absorbed into the mixture.
3. Turn into small jars or moulds and press well
down. Melt the remaining butter and pour over
the top of each mould, while the mixture is still
hot.
4. Leave in the refrigerator at least overnight
before using. **A** **F** Turn out on a plate and serve
with very hot dry toast.

A This will keep for 3 to 4 weeks in the
refrigerator.
F Can be frozen for 3 months. Thaw overnight
in the refrigerator or a cool room, taking care that
the butter does not melt too much.

LITTLE LOAVES WITH SEAFOOD

2 small French loaves
freshly ground black pepper
salt
275 g (10 oz) peeled prawns or crab meat
75 g (3 oz) butter
Forcemeat:
50 g (2 oz) suet
2 teaspoons chopped thyme and parsley
salt
freshly ground black pepper
1 egg
100 g (4 oz) fine white breadcrumbs (may be made
from the inside of the loaves)
1 tablespoon stock (cube will do)

Preparation time: 15 minutes
Cooking time: 15 minutes
Oven: 180°C, 350°F, Gas Mark 4

1. Cut off one end from each loaf and reserve. Scoop out all the crumb.
2. Make the forcemeat by mixing all the ingredients well together.
3. Rub the loaves lightly all over with a grater so that the outside is roughened. Reserve a little of the forcemeat for the ends and spread the remainder on the inside of the loaves. Fill the loaves with the prawns or crab meat. Spread the ends of the loaves with forcemeat and press back into place.
4. Melt the butter in a frying pan and fry the loaves in the hot butter, turning frequently, until a golden brown on all sides. Remove and drain on paper towels.
5. Put the loaves on a baking sheet in a preheated oven for 10 minutes, to heat through. Serve at once, cutting the loaves in half crossways.

From the top, clockwise: *Lobster salad, Little loaves with seafood, Potted shrimps*

87

BAKED RED MULLET IN PORT WINE

Preparation time: 15 minutes
Cooking time: 30 minutes
Oven: 180°C, 350°F, Gas Mark 4

This very delicate fish was much prized in the eighteenth and nineteenth centuries. The gourmet Earl of Arundel used to go specially to Weymouth, where he considered the red mullet were best of all, to eat it every night during its short season. It was served on Feast nights in several Cambridge colleges and this is one of the recipes used.

75 g (3 oz) butter
1 tablespoon finely chopped parsley
1 tablespoon finely chopped shallot
4 red mullet
1 teaspoon anchovy sauce
2 teaspoons Worcestershire sauce
350 ml (12 fl oz) port
40 g (1½ oz) flour
225 g (8 oz) tomatoes, stewed in 300 ml (½ pint)
water and then sieved
1 tablespoon double cream
1 tablespoon milk

1. Well butter a shallow baking dish, and sprinkle with half the parsley and shallot. Lay on the mullet and sprinkle the remainder of the parsley and shallot over them. Pour in the anchovy and Worcestershire sauces and the port.
2. Cover with foil and bake in a preheated oven for 15 minutes, then uncover and bake for a further 10–15 minutes.
3. While the fish is baking, make a roux with the remaining 50 g (2 oz) of butter and the flour. Stir in the puréed tomatoes, the cream and enough milk to give the consistency of very thick cream. Season well and keep warm until the fish are done.
4. Lift the fish on to a warmed serving dish and pour the liquid from the baking dish into the sauce, stirring well.
5. Pour the sauce over the mullet and serve.

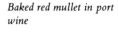

Baked red mullet in port wine

FISH DINNER FROM YARMOUTH

In the early years of this century a visitor to Yarmouth wrote down this recipe for a delicious fish dinner, unlike any other she had ever had. The wives of the fishermen used to go to the quay and collect the broken fish that were left after the catch had been sorted for the fish market. The women went home and made this meal with their own variations, such as cheese sprinkled on the fish.

Serves 6
50 g (2 oz) butter
2 large onions, peeled and finely chopped
3 mackerel, cleaned and filleted
1 teaspoon ground mace
½ teaspoon turmeric
salt
pepper
750 g (1½ lb) haddock, hake or cod fillets
900 ml (1½ pints) cold water
225 g (8 oz) crab meat
3 tablespoons chopped parsley

Preparation time: 10 minutes
Cooking time: 25 minutes

1. Melt the butter in a large pan and fry the onions until just soft but not coloured.
2. Lay the fillets of mackerel on top of the onions and sprinkle with half the spices and a pinch of salt and pepper.
3. Add the haddock, hake or cod fillets and sprinkle on the remaining spices. Pour on the cold water. Bring to the boil and simmer very gently for 20 minutes.
4. Lift out the fish fillets and the onion with a perforated spoon, reserving the cooking liquid.
5. Arrange the fish in a large, shallow, ovenproof dish. (It does not matter if some pieces are broken.) Flake the crab meat and spread it on top of the fish.
6. Pour a little of the cooking liquid around and over the fish. Cover with foil and keep hot.
7. Adjust the seasoning of the remaining stock and serve in bowls with crusty bread, followed by the fish, thickly sprinkled with parsley and served with boiled potatoes with butter.

Fish dinner from Yarmouth

NORFOLK POTTAGE
WITH GREEN DUMPLINGS

A very good supper party dish, this pottage comes from an anonymous cookery book which dates from the eighteenth century. The original recipe, intended for a feast day, would serve about 40 people. It calls for a whole leg of beef, a large piece of veal, half a pound of bacon, 4 ox palates, 4 sweetbreads, 2 dozen cockscombs, several fowls, 24 pints of water and various herbs and spices.

Translated into reasonable quantities and replacing the palates, sweetbreads and cockscombs with kidneys, it remains a most excellent, strong and subtly flavoured stew, with an inimitable, rich, thick gravy. It is often served with dumplings. You will require 2 large, heavy saucepans.

Serves 8–10
2 medium onions, peeled and cut in rings
450 g (1 lb) carrots, scraped and diced into
1 cm ($\frac{1}{2}$ inch) cubes
1 chicken, about 1.25 kg (2$\frac{1}{2}$ lb)
salt
pepper
$\frac{1}{2}$ teaspoon ground mace
2 sprigs thyme or 1 teaspoon dried thyme
2 tablespoons lemon juice
1 kg (2 lb) stewing steak, cut in thin slices
2 bacon rashers, finely chopped
6 lamb's kidneys or 350 g (12 oz) ox kidney,
skinned, cored and sliced
350 g (12 oz) mushrooms
6 large canned artichoke hearts, cut in quarters
90 g (3$\frac{1}{2}$ oz) butter
450 g (1 lb) shelled peas
1 kg (2 lb) new potatoes, scrubbed
50 g (2 oz) plain flour
Green dumplings:
225 g (8 oz) self-raising flour, plus extra for
sprinkling
75 g (3 oz) suet
1 teaspoon salt
1$\frac{1}{2}$ tablespoons finely chopped parsley
150 ml ($\frac{1}{4}$ pint) milk and water mixed

Preparation time: 30 minutes
Cooking time: 1$\frac{3}{4}$ hours

---

1. In the bottom of each saucepan, put half the onion rings and half the carrots.
2. In one saucepan place the whole chicken. Barely cover with water, adding 1 teaspoon salt, $\frac{1}{2}$ teaspoon of pepper, half the mace, 1 sprig thyme, and $\frac{1}{2}$ tablespoon lemon juice.
3. In the second pan put the steak, bacon and kidneys, cover with water and repeat the seasoning.

4. Stew both very gently, closely covered, for 1$\frac{1}{2}$ hours.
5. Mix the flour, suet, salt and parsley in a bowl, and stir in the liquid gradually to make a stiff dough. Sprinkle some flour on a plate and roll small balls of the dough – about 2.5 cm (1 inch) in diameter – in the flour.
6. After cooking the meat for 1 hour, add half the mushrooms and half the dumplings to each pan, laying the dumplings carefully on top of the meat.
7. Meanwhile, cook the remaining vegetables. Fry the artichoke hearts in 40 g (1$\frac{1}{2}$ oz) of the butter for 3 minutes each side, and boil the peas and new potatoes separately until tender. Keep the vegetables warm.
8. Remove both saucepans from the heat. Lift out the dumplings into a serving dish and keep warm. Lift the chicken out, remove the skin and take all the meat off the bones, leaving it in large pieces. Take out the meat from the second saucepan and arrange on a very large flat serving dish, with the chicken pieces. The vegetables from both saucepans should be lifted out of the stock with a perforated spoon and arranged among the pieces of meat. Keep hot while finishing the gravy.
9. Combine the stocks from the two saucepans. Make a roux with the remaining butter and the flour, stir in a little of the stock and bring to the boil. Gradually add more stock until you have about 1 litre (1$\frac{3}{4}$ pints) of gravy, the consistency of thin cream. Check the seasoning and add the remaining lemon juice and some freshly ground black pepper.
10. Pour the gravy over the meats on the dish and serve at once with the potatoes, peas and artichokes arranged as a border. The dumplings can also be arranged around the serving dish, or served separately.

Norfolk pottage with Green dumplings

FILLETS OF PORK

A delicious rich recipe for a special occasion. The cream and butter can be replaced by 150 ml (¼ pint) milk and 100 g (4 oz) margarine, for a plainer dish if preferred.

225 g (8 oz) large prunes, soaked for 3 hours, stoned and finely chopped, reserving the soaking liquid
75 g (3 oz) white breadcrumbs
1 tablespoon finely chopped onion, softened in a little butter
2 fillets of pork, each about 350 g (12 oz), trimmed and halved crosswise
40 g (1½ oz) flour, plus 2 tablespoons seasoned flour
salt
pepper
75 g (3 oz) butter
150 ml (¼ pint) good white stock (a bouillon cube will do)
150 ml (¼ pint) double cream
1 tablespoon brandy

Preparation time: 20 minutes, plus soaking
Cooking time: 55 minutes
Oven: 180°C, 350°F, Gas Mark 4

1. Mix the prunes with the breadcrumbs and onion.
2. Split each fillet in half lengthways. Spread the lower halves with the prune filling, then replace the top halves, like long sandwiches. Tie securely at intervals with fine twine.
3. Rub the stuffed fillets with seasoned flour and place in a shallow ovenproof dish. Melt the butter and pour over. Bake, tightly covered, for 40 minutes in a preheated oven.
4. Remove the fillets from the oven and pour off the butter and juices into a small pan. Return the pork fillets to the oven, uncovered, to bake for a further 15 minutes, so that the tops are lightly browned. Remove the strings.
5. Make the sauce by stirring the flour into the butter and pork juices and then adding the prune juice and the stock. Boil for 3 minutes.
6. Stir in the cream and then the brandy. Do not allow to boil again, but keep warm until the fillets are ready.
7. Pour the sauce round the pork and serve immediately.

SALMI OF DUCK

Until the end of the nineteenth century, wild duck were so plentiful in the fens and marshes of East Anglia that a salmi made a pleasant alternative to the traditional plain roast. The birds are roasted very rare a short time before they are wanted and then put into a sauce, in which they are gently heated. This recipe is rather complicated to prepare but well worth the trouble. It is equally good with pheasant or partridge. The sauce is rich and splendid.

Serves 4–6
2 ducks or 3 wild ducks, roasted for 30 minutes only and allowed to cool
1 medium onion, peeled and finely chopped
40 g (1½ oz) butter
1 tablespoon plain flour
1 teaspoon dried thyme
1 teaspoon dried parsley

From the left: *Fillets of pork, Salmi of duck*

2 bay leaves
¼ teaspoon grated nutmeg
grated rind of 1 orange
2 teaspoons redcurrant jelly
salt
pepper
150 ml (¼ pint) red wine
1 tablespoon brandy
100 g (4 oz) mushrooms, sliced and lightly fried in butter
2 teaspoons lemon juice

Preparation time: 45 minutes
Cooking time: 2½ hours

1. Carve all the meat from the ducks, the breast in long slices, the rest as you can get it away from the bone. Set aside in the refrigerator.
2. Put the bones in a saucepan, just cover with salted water and boil for at least 1½ hours. Strain off the stock.
3. Fry the onion in the butter until just transpa- rent and golden. Stir in the flour, cook for a minute and gradually stir in the stock. Add the herbs, the nutmeg and the grated orange rind and stir in the redcurrant jelly. Season with salt and pepper and simmer for 30 minutes, uncovered, stirring occasionally, until the sauce is as thick as double cream.
4. Strain the sauce through a sieve into another saucepan, add the wine, brandy and mushrooms and simmer for 5 or 6 minutes. Add the lemon juice.
5. Check the seasoning and add the pieces of duck. Leave on the lowest possible heat for another 15 minutes, so that the duck is heated through, but do not allow it to boil.
6. Pour into a serving dish and serve immedi- ately.

GAME PIE

Oven: 150°C, 300°F, Gas Mark 2
then: 200°C, 400°F, Gas Mark 6
then: 150°C, 300°F, Gas Mark 2

A traditional East Anglian game pie, which is also excellent cold, particularly if raised pie pastry, which is intended to be eaten cold, is used.

25 g (1 oz) butter
1 large onion, peeled and finely chopped
2 partridges or 1 other small game bird or 1 pheasant, cleaned and jointed
225 g (8 oz) lean steak, cut into 2.5 cm (1 inch) pieces
2 rashers bacon, rinded and cut into 1 cm (½ inch) strips
100 g (4 oz) mushrooms
1 sprig thyme
1 bay leaf
salt
freshly ground black pepper
600 ml (1 pint) brown stock
275 g (10 oz) shortcrust (page 99) or flaky (page 61) pastry or for a cold pie 275 g (10 oz) raised pie pastry (page 96)
1 egg, beaten

Preparation time: 30 minutes, plus cooling
Cooking time: 2¼–2¾ hours

Game pie

1. Melt the butter in a frying pan, add the onion and cook until softened. Add the game and brown on all sides. Remove from the pan and reserve.
2. Add the steak and brown lightly.
3. Spread the steak on the bottom of a large pie dish and arrange the joints on top. Sprinkle the onion, bacon, mushrooms and herbs on top. Season to taste. Just cover with stock, cover with foil and simmer in the preheated oven until tender, about 1½–2 hours.
4. Remove the dish from the oven and allow to cool. Heat the oven to the higher temperature. Add a little more stock to bring the liquid to 1 cm (½ inch) from the top of the meat.
5. Roll out the pastry and cut out a lid to fit the dish. Cut a strip 2.5 cm (1 inch) wide and lay on the rim of the dish. Moisten with water, then lay on the pastry lid, pressing it down firmly. Knock back the edges and mark with a knife in ridges. Brush with beaten egg. Roll out the trimmings and use to make leaves or other decorations. Place on the lid and brush with egg again. Bake in a preheated oven for 20 minutes.
6. Reduce the oven heat, place the pie lower in the oven and bake for a further 15–20 minutes.

HONEY ROASTED TURKEY WITH CANDIED POTATOES

— ∽ —

Turkeys, until the middle of this century, were most successfully bred in Norfolk. In the seventeenth century they were taken to the London markets on foot, in great droves of 500 or more. Even though there were no hard roads, their feet often became sore and a good drover would pen them up in some market town and bind up their feet in rags to protect them. At the end of the journey they had to be fattened up for a few days before they could be sold. This way of cooking them, which is unsurpassed, comes from Norfolk.

The potatoes will be deliciously candied from the honey, while taking up the flavour of the turkey from the juice. Gravy should be made separately, from the giblets, as the honey in the pan makes it too sweet.

Serves 8–10
225 g (8 oz) medium thick honey
100 g (4 oz) butter
3.5–5.5 kg (8–12 lb) turkey
1.4 kg (3 lb) potatoes, peeled and halved

Allow 15 minutes roasting per 450 g (1 lb)
Preparation time: 5 minutes, plus standing
Oven: 200°C, 400°F, Gas Mark 6;
then: 180°C, 350°F, Gas Mark 4

1. Melt the honey and butter together and stir well. Place the turkey in a roasting tin and pour the mixture all over it. Allow to stand for an hour or so, basting occasionally with the mixture which has run off into the tray.

2. Arrange the potatoes around the turkey and roast in a preheated oven for 40 minutes. The honey will make an almost black crust over the bird, sealing in the flavour. Baste with the mixture that has run off and reduce the oven heat.

3. Return to the oven for a further 30 minutes, then baste again. Cover the turkey with foil and continue cooking.

4. 15 minutes before serving, remove the foil so that the skin may crisp.

Honey roasted turkey with candied potatoes

95

VEGETABLE PIE WITH POTATO PASTRY

This is a very old recipe, originally designed for fast days when meat was forbidden by the Church.

Pastry:
175 g (6 oz) butter or soft margarine
225 g (8 oz) self-raising flour
1 teaspoon salt
225 g (8 oz) cold, cooked mashed potato
1 tablespoon milk
1 beaten egg yolk
Filling:
225 g (8 oz) mixed vegetables, either frozen or fresh diced, cooked until just tender and allowed to cool
100 g (4 oz) mushrooms, sliced, lightly fried and allowed to cool
1 large or 2 medium onions, peeled, finely sliced, lightly fried and allowed to cool
150 ml ($\frac{1}{4}$ pint) white sauce (see below)
salt
pepper
75 g (3 oz) grated cheddar cheese

Preparation time: 30 minutes, plus cooling time
Cooking time: 30 minutes
Oven: 200°C, 400°F, Gas Mark 6

1. Rub the butter into the flour, stir in the salt and work this mixture into the mashed potato, adding the milk a little at a time.
2. Knead on a floured board until the dough is smooth and fairly soft. Roll out the pastry and use to line a large, shallow, ovenproof dish. Bake blind in a preheated, moderately hot oven for 15 minutes or until it is a light golden brown.
3. While the pastry is cooking, mix all the vegetables into the sauce and season to taste.
4. Remove the pastry from the oven, allow to cool a little and then fill with the vegetable mixture, spreading with a palette knife so that it is smooth and flat. Sprinkle with the grated cheese.
5. Brush the edges of the pastry with the beaten egg yolk and return to the oven for 15 minutes or until the cheese is melted and beginning to brown.

WHITE SAUCE
25 g (1 oz) butter
25 g (1 oz) plain flour
600 ml (1 pint) milk
salt
pepper

Melt the butter in a small heavy saucepan, being careful not to let it colour. Add the flour and cook for 1 minute, stirring. Gradually add the milk and bring to the boil, stirring. Season with salt and pepper and remove from the heat.

SUFFOLK HAM TOASTS

Serves 6
12 eggs
salt
freshly ground black pepper
6 slices white bread
100 g (4 oz) butter
2 tablespoons double cream
225–350 g (8–12 oz) lean ham or gammon (home-cooked if possible), finely chopped or minced in a food processor

Preparation time: 5 minutes
Cooking time: 15 minutes

1. Beat the eggs well with $\frac{1}{4}$ teaspoon salt and $\frac{1}{4}$ teaspoon freshly ground black pepper.
2. Toast the bread and cut off the crusts. Using about half the butter, butter each slice and keep it warm in a very low oven. Melt the remainder of the butter in a heavy saucepan and reserve.
3. Put the cream in a very small saucepan, stir in the ham and $\frac{1}{4}$ teaspoon of black pepper. Stir over a low heat until warmed through. Spread the cream mixture over the hot buttered toasts and return to the oven to keep hot.
4. Re-heat the melted butter and stir in the beaten eggs. Continue to stir until the eggs are just on the point of setting. Immediately take the toasts out of the oven and spoon the scrambled egg on to each one. Serve at once.

LITTLE MUTTON PIES

In 1805 a large platter of these pies was served at a dinner given by the Marquis of Buckingham.

Makes 8 pies
150 ml ($\frac{1}{4}$ pint) red wine, boiled until reduced by one-third
300 ml ($\frac{1}{2}$ pint) brown stock
350 g (12 oz) lean lamb from the fillet end of a leg, finely chopped
1 medium onion, peeled and finely chopped
225 g (8 oz) mushrooms, finely chopped
1 teaspoon dried thyme
salt
freshly ground black pepper
450 g (1 lb) raised pie pastry (see below) or flaky pastry (page 61)
1 egg, beaten
Pastry:
225 g (8 oz) lard (or half lard and half butter)
450 g (1 lb) plain flour
1 teaspoon salt
150 ml ($\frac{1}{4}$ pint) milk and water (half and half)

From the top:
Vegetable pie with
potato pastry, Suffolk
ham toasts, Little mutton
pies

Preparation time: 40 minutes (including pastry)
Cooking time: 1¼ hours
Oven: 190°C, 375°F, Gas Mark 5

1. Stir the reduced wine into the stock, add the meat, onion, mushrooms, thyme and seasoning and simmer very gently for 40 minutes. Pour off the gravy and reserve. Leave the meat to get cold.
2. To make the raised pie pastry, rub 50 g (2 oz) of the fat into the flour and add a teaspoon of salt.
3. Put the milk and water in a saucepan, add the rest of the fat and bring to the boil. Make a well in the flour, pour in the boiling liquid and stir thoroughly with a wooden spoon. When it is well mixed, knead the pastry and then allow to stand for 10 minutes. It should still be warm and pliable.
4. Divide the pastry into 8 equal pieces and roll out each piece 1–2 cm (½–¾ inch) thick. Using a 9 cm (3½ in) individual soufflé dish, stand the dish in the middle of a pastry round and work the pastry up to cover the sides. Turn the pastry-

covered dish on its side and roll it a few times to smooth the outside and loosen the dish. Gently work the dish out and the little pie shell will remain standing. Trim the top to even it with a sharp knife. Repeat with the other pastry rounds. Roll out all the trimmings and use to cut out 8 lids, a little bigger than the diameter of the pies. If using flaky pastry, line 8 small soufflé dishes with the pastry and cut out and reserve 8 lids.
5. Remove the grease from the top of the cold gravy. Fill the pies with the meat mixture and put a spoonful of gravy into each one.
6. Put the lids on the pies, crimping the edges to make a ridge all round, and make a small hole in the centre of each. Brush with the beaten egg.
7. Bake the pies in a preheated oven for 35 minutes, or until the pastry is crisp and golden brown. If using flaky pastry, work the pies very carefully out of the dishes. Heat the reserved gravy and pour a little through the hole in the top of each pie.

SUFFOLK CAKES

The recipe for these very light but rich-tasting little cakes, very quick and easy to make, comes from a nineteenth century manuscript of recipes collected for her own use by a certain Mrs. Anstey, cook to several well-to-do families in Suffolk.

Makes about 14 cakes
100 g (4 oz) butter
4 eggs
225 g (8 oz) caster sugar
grated zest of $\frac{1}{2}$ lemon
100 g (4 oz) self-raising flour

Preparation time: 10 minutes
Cooking time: 15 minutes
Oven: 200°C, 400°F, Gas Mark 6

1. Warm the butter so that it is just liquid but not at all coloured.
2. Separate the eggs and beat the whites till they just hold a peak.
3. Beat the yolks, add the sugar and grated lemon zest and fold into the beaten whites.
4. Beat in the butter and stir in the flour. Beat well and turn into greased bun tins or patty pans.
5. Bake in a preheated oven for 10–15 minutes.

VINEGAR CAKE

An old Norfolk farmhouse recipe for a good, plain fruit cake that will keep for a week. The flavour improves all the time. The recipe needs no eggs and probably was originally made when the hens were not laying.

Makes one 23 cm (9 inch) cake
225 g (8 oz) butter
450 g (1 lb) plain flour
225 g (8 oz) sugar
225 g (8 oz) raisins
225 g (8 oz) sultanas
250 ml (8 fl oz) milk
2 tablespoons wine or cider vinegar
1 teaspoon bicarbonate of soda mixed with
1 tablespoon milk

Preparation time: 10 minutes
Cooking time: $1\frac{3}{4}$ hours
Oven: 180°C, 350°F, Gas Mark 4
then: 150°C, 300°F, Gas Mark 2

1. Rub the butter into the flour to give a crumb-like consistency. Mix in the sugar and the fruit.
2. Put the milk into a large jug or bowl and add the vinegar.

3. Pour the bicarbonate of soda and milk mixture into the milk and vinegar. It will froth up and may overflow, so it is wise to hold it over the mixing bowl while doing this.
4. Stir the liquid into the cake mixture, beat well and put into a well-greased 23 cm (9 inch) tin.
5. Put in a preheated oven and bake for 30 minutes. Then reduce heat and bake for a further $1\frac{1}{4}$ hours, lightly covering the top of the cake with foil if it starts to darken too much.

THE PRIOR'S SWEET OMELETTE

It is recorded that the Prior of an ancient monastery near the Norfolk coast preferred dishes made with milk and honey to those made with meat and game. This early recipe was the kind of dish that was served to him.

Serves 2
4 eggs, separated
1 orange
2 tablespoons double cream
1 tablespoon clear honey
15 g ($\frac{1}{2}$ oz) butter

Preparation time: 10 minutes
Cooking time: 3 minutes

1. Beat the egg yolks well, and the whites so that they hold a peak.
2. Cut the orange in half and cut one half across again. Grate the zest, squeeze the juice from the half orange and set both aside.
3. Whip the cream till it thickens and stands, but do not over beat. Fold the honey and the orange juice into the cream and refrigerate until required.
4. Melt the butter in an omelette pan until sizzling. Fold the egg whites into the yolks and pour into the pan. Turn the edge inwards from the edge of the pan as it cooks. In 2 minutes only the centre will be soft.
5. Immediately spoon the cream and honey mixture on to the omelette, a little off-centre, so that one half of the omelette can be folded over it.
6. Lift quickly, but carefully on to a hot dish. Sprinkle the orange zest over it and garnish with the remaining orange quarters.

APPLE FLORENTINE PIE

An eighteenth century recipe from Lincolnshire and Bedfordshire, traditionally made at Christmas.

4 large cooking apples
3 tablespoons demerara sugar
1 tablespoon grated lemon peel
50 g (2 oz) sultanas
600 ml (1 pint) pale ale
¼ teaspoon grated nutmeg
¼ teaspoon cinnamon
3 cloves
whipped cream, to serve
Shortcrust pastry
¼ teaspoon salt
225 g (8 oz) plain flour
100 g (4 oz) butter or margarine
50 ml (2 fl oz) very cold water

Preparation time: 30 minutes
Cooking time: 30 minutes
Oven: 200°C, 400°F, Gas Mark 6

1. Make the pastry by mixing the salt and flour lightly together and rubbing in the butter until it is the consistency of fine breadcrumbs. Mix with the cold water until a soft dough is formed. Roll out to 1 cm (½ inch) thick on a floured board.

2. Peel and core the apples, stand in a deep, buttered pie dish and sprinkle with 2 tablespoons of the sugar and 1 teaspoon of grated lemon peel. Fill the centre of each apple with sultanas.

3. Cover with the pastry and bake in a preheated oven for 30 minutes.

4. Heat together, but do not boil, the ale, nutmeg, cinnamon, cloves and remaining sugar.

5. Carefully loosen the crust and lift the pastry off the apples. Pour the ale mixture over the apples. Cut the pastry into 4 pieces and place one on each apple.

6. Serve very hot in bowls. Whipped cream is delicious with this.

From the top, clockwise: *Suffolk cakes, Vinegar cake, Apple florentine pies, The prior's sweet omelette*

The WEST COUNTRY

Devon, Cornwall, Dorset, Somerset, Wiltshire, Gloucestershire

The West Country, more than any other region, has always had a strong sea-going connection. The great seafarers of Devon and Bristol in the 16th, 17th, and 18th centuries ensured that foods from other parts of the world, such as the potato, turkeys and spices, became available to all, instead of just the few who could afford the high prices paid for them.

The warm climate engendered by the Gulf Stream makes the West Country one of the richest and most fertile of lands: it is ideal for fruit and flower growing, and provides lush grazing for sheep and cattle. Old breeds of pigs, such as Gloucester Old Spots, still root in the apple orchards which give us such excellent cider. World-famous cheeses, much imitated, such as Cheddar and Double Gloucester, also play their part in this bountiful part of England. Many of the local dishes are cooked with the plentiful herbs, golden butter and clotted cream unique to the West Country.

In addition to these fine foods, there are excellent fish and shellfish, such as crab, which is to be found in many restaurants, and even in pubs in freshly-cut sandwiches. There is hake, fine salmon, sole – that from Torbay is highly thought of – and large scallops. It all adds up to a delicious array of foods for all occasions from the dramatic 'Stargazey pie' to the luxury of a real cream tea, with Devon splits, strawberry jam and clotted cream.

'There was meals, roasted chickens, an' a tongue, an' a great ham. There was cheesecakes that she made after a little secret of her own; an' a bowl of junket an inch deep in cream, that bein' his pet dish.'
Arthur Quiller-Couch, 1863–1944, *Q's Shorter Stories*

St Mawes, Cornwall

CRAB SOUP

Crabs are found all round the coast but especially in Cornwall from where many recipes originate. This soup is delicious and extremely filling. If possible add a few strands of saffron, which will give it not only a gorgeous golden colour, but also a honey-like taste.

Serves 6
225 g (8 oz) fresh or frozen crab meat
50 g (2 oz) butter
50 g (2 oz) plain flour
900 ml (1½ pints) creamy milk
1.2 litres (2 pints) chicken stock
salt
white pepper
¼ teaspoon nutmeg
a few strands of saffron (optional)
2 tablespoons dry sherry
150 ml (¼ pint) double or whipping cream

Preparation time: 5 minutes
Cooking time: 20 minutes

1. Separate the white and dark crab meat.
2. Heat the butter until foaming, stir in the flour and let it cook for a minute, then add the milk, stirring well, then the chicken stock. Add the dark crab meat, salt, pepper and nutmeg and simmer gently for about 12–15 minutes. Add the saffron, if liked, stir, and then put in the white crab meat and the sherry.
3. Bring to just under boiling point, simmer for 5 minutes and taste for seasoning.
4. Transfer to a soup tureen as it is, with a swirl of cream, or it may be sieved or blended if liked.

WHITE FOAM SOUP

This soup is traditional to Gloucestershire. It is extremely light and good.

Serves 6–8
40 g (1½ oz) butter
50 g (2 oz) plain flour
2.25 litres (4 pints) milk, warmed
1 large garlic clove, crushed
1 medium onion, peeled and sliced
2 celery sticks, chopped
small piece of mace blade
2 eggs, separated
salt
pepper
50 g (2 oz) hard cheese, grated
finely chopped parsley, to garnish

Preparation time: 15 minutes
Cooking time: 40 minutes

1. Heat the butter, stir in the flour and cook for a minute, then add the milk gradually, stirring all the time until smooth. Simmer gently, then add the crushed garlic, onion, celery and mace. Cover and simmer for about 30 minutes.
2. Cool slightly, then carefully stir in the well-beaten egg yolks. Return to the heat but do not allow to boil. Taste for seasoning.
3. Add the grated cheese, stirring well, and keep warm. Beat the egg whites until stiff but not dry, fold half into the soup and put the rest into the tureen or soup bowls and pour the hot soup over. Garnish with a little chopped parsley.

MUSSEL AND CIDER SOUP

Serves 4–6
1.5–1.75 kg (3–4 lb) fresh mussels
1.2 litres (2 pints) dry cider
50 g (2 oz) butter
50 g (2 oz) plain flour
3 celery sticks, chopped
1 small onion, peeled and chopped
salt
pepper
300 ml (½ pint) single cream
To garnish:
chopped parsley

Preparation time: 40 minutes
Cooking time: 25 minutes

1. Wash and scrub the mussels to get rid of sand or grit, discarding all that are open. Then put into a large saucepan with the cider. Cover and bring to the boil, then cook for about 5 minutes, shaking the pan, until they are all open. Leave to cool a little, then strain but reserve the liquor.
2. When cool enough, take the mussels from their shells and remove the beards.
3. Heat the butter, add the flour and let it cook for a minute, then gradually add the mussel stock, stirring until it boils and is smooth and creamy.
4. Add the finely chopped celery and onion to the thickened stock and cook until they are quite tender.
5. Taste for seasoning, add the cream and finally the mussels. Heat gently, but do not allow to reboil. Serve with a garnish of parsley.

From the bottom, clockwise: *Mussel and cider soup, White foam soup, Crab soup, Cornish pasties (page 105)*

LEEK OR LIKKY PIE

225 g (8 oz) flaky pastry (page 61)
6 large leeks, washed, trimmed and cut into 1 cm
(½ inch) lengths
2 eggs, beaten
150 ml (¼ pint) double or whipping cream
150 ml (¼ pint) milk
100 g (4 oz) streaky bacon or pork, rinded and finely
chopped
salt
freshly ground black pepper

Preparation time: 30 minutes, plus chilling
Cooking time: 45 minutes
Oven: 200°C, 400°F, Gas Mark 6

1. Chill the pastry for 30–40 minutes.
2. Put the leeks into boiling salted water and cook for about 7 minutes, then drain well.
3. Reserve a little of the egg for glazing, then beat in the rest with the cream and milk.
4. Put the leeks, bacon, eggs and cream into a deep pie dish and season to taste.
5. Dampen the edges of the pie dish, roll out the pastry to the size of the dish and put on top, pinching the edges well. Brush over with a little beaten egg and bake for about half an hour.

PARSON'S HAT

This is a Devonshire version of the pasty.

225 g (8 oz) shortcrust pastry (page 99)
4 tablespoons white sauce, or 2 eggs beaten with
4 tablespoons milk
175 g (6 oz) cooked haddock, salmon, cod, etc.
pinch of cayenne pepper
salt
freshly ground black pepper
1 tablespoon grated Cheddar cheese
milk, for brushing

Preparation time: 45 minutes, plus chilling
Cooking time: 30 minutes
Oven: 190°C, 375°F, Gas Mark 5

1. Chill the pastry for 30–40 minutes.
2. Put the sauce or egg mixture into a basin. Take all the skin and bones from the fish and mix with the sauce or egg. Season well with cayenne, salt and pepper, and add the cheese.
3. Roll out the pastry fairly thinly and cut into 8–10 cm (3–4 inch) circles. Brush with a little of the egg and milk and divide the filling between the rounds. Slightly dampen the edges and press upwards into a three-cornered shape with a little filling showing at the top.

4. Put on to a slightly greased baking tray and brush over with a little milk. Place in a preheated oven and bake for about half an hour.

PRIDDY OGGIES

Oggie is a West Country name for pastry. Priddy oggies, with a meat and cheese filling, were first served at The Miner's Arms, Priddy in Somerset. They are both original and delicious, being first baked, then deep-fried.

Makes 8
25 g (1 oz) butter
25 g (1 oz) lard
1 small egg yolk
90 g (3½ oz) Cheddar cheese, grated
2½ tablespoons water
pinch of salt
225 g (8 oz) plain flour, sifted
600 ml (1 pint) vegetable oil, for deep frying
Filling:
500 g (1¼ lb) pork fillet
1 egg, beaten
75 g (3 oz) mature Cheddar cheese, grated
2 tablespoons chopped parsley
pinch of salt
a little cayenne pepper
40 g (1½ oz) smoked bacon, cut into 8 strips

Preparation time: 60 minutes, plus chilling
Cooking time: about 25 minutes
Oven: 200°C, 400°F, Gas Mark 6

1. To make the pastry, mix all the ingredients except the flour in a warm bowl until soft. Cool the mixture in a refrigerator until it is firm. Sieve the flour and rub in the cooled mixture roughly.
2. Divide the mixture into thirds. Take each piece and roll it 2 or 3 times into a 1 cm (½ inch) slab, moistening the top of each slab slightly before laying them on top of each other. When finished, press down firmly and cut downwards into 3 pieces, repeating the rolling process twice more. Chill for 30 minutes.
3. Trim the fillet and slice lengthways into 2, then beat gently until flat.
4. Reserve half the beaten egg, then place the cheese, parsley, salt and cayenne in the bowl with the rest of the egg and mix well.
5. Spread the mixture evenly over the cut sides of the pork fillet, then roll up each piece, pressing down firmly. Chill for 30 minutes.
6. To assemble the oggies, cut each roll of fillet into 4 slices and wrap them round with a piece of bacon. Roll out the pastry and cut into 8 equal squares. Lay a slice of the stuffed meat in the centre of the pastry, then moisten around the edges with a little water. Bring the pastry up and over the

meat, pressing the edges together in a scalloped design. Press down the base slightly to flatten. Put onto a baking sheet and when all are ready brush over with the remaining beaten egg.

7. Place the oggies in the centre of the preheated oven and bake for about 15 minutes, or until they are just starting to brown.

8. Heat the oil in a deep fryer to 180°C/350°F, or until a cube of bread browns in 30 seconds. Deep-fry the oggies until the pastry begins to brown, then drain on paper towels.

CORNISH PASTY

The traditional Cornish pasty is made with good shortcrust pastry and filled with meat and vegetables. The meat should be raw, not minced, but finely chopped by hand, and the vegetables coarsely grated so that they all cook at the same time.

¼ teaspoon salt
450 g (1 lb) plain flour
225 g (8 oz) margarine
6 tablespoons iced water
450 g (1 lb) finely chopped lean beef or lamb
225 g (8 oz) potatoes, peeled and grated
1 small piece of turnip or swede, grated
3–4 tablespoons cold water

salt
freshly ground black pepper
a little milk or egg to glaze

Preparation time: 1 hour, plus chilling
Cooking time: 55 minutes to 1 hour
Oven: 220°C, 425°F, Gas Mark 7
then: 180°C, 350°F, Gas Mark 4

1. First make the pastry by sifting the salt and flour, then rubbing in the fat with the fingers until it is like coarse breadcrumbs. Add enough iced water gradually to make a stiff dough, kneading lightly with your hands until it is smooth. Wrap up in polythene and chill for at least 30 minutes.

2. Mix the meat and vegetables together with the water and season very well.

3. Roll out the pastry on a floured surface to about 5 mm (¼ inch) thick and cut into 4 circles about 20 cm (8 inches) in diameter.

4. Divide the mixture between the 4 circles, filling only one half of the circle. Dampen the edges with cold water, fold over to cover mixture and press with a fork or the fingers to make it secure. (Or put the filling in the middle and draw up the edges to the centre top.)

5. Brush over the pasties with milk or a little beaten egg, and make a small slit on top. Put them on to a greased baking sheet and bake in a preheated oven for 15 minutes, then reduce the oven temperature and bake for about 35–40 minutes. Serve hot or cold.

From the top, clockwise: *Leek or likky pie, Priddy oggies, Parson's hat*

Baked scallops

BAKED SCALLOPS

Scallops have such a delicate flavour that the cheese often served with them can mask the flavour. This West Country method of baking them enhances their flavour.

8–10 scallops with their shells
salt
freshly ground black pepper
100 g (4 oz) butter
4 tablespoons fresh breadcrumbs

Preparation time: 30 minutes
Cooking time: 30 minutes
Oven: 180°C, 350°F, Gas Mark 4

1. Take the scallops from the shell with a sharp knife. Cut off or discard the black part. Then chop the white flesh coarsely, leaving the orange coral whole. Reserve the rounded part of 4 shells and scrub or wash thoroughly.
2. Divide the chopped scallops and coral evenly between the 4 shells and season to taste. Dot the scallops with 50 g (2 oz) butter.
3. Sprinkle the fresh breadcrumbs equally between the shells and use the remaining butter to dot over the tops.
4. Cook in the middle of the preheated oven for about 30 minutes, or until the top is crisp and bubbly and the scallops cooked.

BAKED MACKEREL WITH RHUBARB SAUCE

This dish is a speciality of Bristol where the fishermen would be served this for supper.

4 mackerel, cleaned and filleted
4 bay leaves
12 black peppercorns
300 ml ($\frac{1}{2}$ pint) dry cider
225 g (8 oz) prepared rhubarb
4 tablespoons cider
1 teaspoon lemon juice
pinch of ground mace
pinch of ground cinnamon
2 tablespoons butter

Preparation time: 15 minutes
Cooking time: 30–40 minutes
Oven: 180°C, 350°F, Gas Mark 4

1. Put the mackerel fillets into an ovenproof dish with a bay leaf on each, then scatter the peppercorns around.
2. Barely cover the fish with cider and bake in the preheated oven for about 30–40 minutes. When cooked, keep hot.
3. Put the rhubarb and all the other ingredients except the butter into a small saucepan. Cook until puréed. Before serving, add the butter in pieces so that it melts through the hot purée.

STARGAZEY PIE

This Cornish pie is probably so called because the fishes' heads are left outside the pastry, gazing upwards. Originally they were arranged like this because the oil drained back into the pie, so nothing was wasted. In some parts of Cornwall a mashed potato crust is used instead of pastry.

Serves 4–6
6 tablespoons fresh white breadcrumbs
150 ml ($\frac{1}{4}$ pint) milk
2 tablespoons chopped parsley
3 tablespoons lemon juice
grated rind of 1 lemon
1 medium onion, peeled and chopped
6 pilchards, herrings or mackerel, cleaned and filleted, with the heads left on (ask the fishmonger to do this)
2 hard-boiled eggs, chopped
1 rasher bacon, rinded and chopped
salt
freshly ground black pepper
150ml ($\frac{1}{4}$ pint) dry cider
225 g (8 oz) puff or flaky pastry (page 61)

Preparation time: 40 minutes
Cooking time: 40 minutes
Oven: 220°C, 425°F, Gas Mark 7
then: 190°C, 375°F, Gas Mark 5

1. To make the stuffing, soak the breadcrumbs in the milk and leave to swell a little.
2. Add the parsley, lemon juice and rind and onion and mix well.
3. Divide the stuffing between the fish, spreading it on the flat fillets. Fold them over, then put into a round ovenproof pie dish, tails downwards and with the heads on the edge.
4. Put the chopped eggs, chopped bacon, seasoning and cider all around and in between the fish.
5. Roll out the pastry to fit the dish. Press on, leaving the fish heads exposed on the rim.
6. Bake in the preheated oven for 15 minutes, then reduce the oven temperature and cook for a further 25 minutes.

From the left: *Baked mackerel with rhubarb sauce, Stargazey pie*

HAKE WITH LEMON BUTTER SAUCE

A lot of hake is caught off the Devon coast. It is a delicious fish with a slightly pink coloured flesh.

4 thick hake cutlets
Court bouillon:
white fish heads, bones and skin
1 small onion, chopped
1 teaspoon grated lemon rind
6 black peppercorns
sprig of parsley or fennel
900 ml (1½ pints) water, or half white wine and half water
Sauce:
175 g (6 oz) butter
2 tablespoons cornflour
2 tablespoons lemon juice
salt
freshly ground black pepper
lemon twist
sprig of fennel

Preparation time: 15 minutes
Cooking time: 45 minutes

1. First make the court bouillon by putting the fish bones and skin into a saucepan with all the other ingredients. Boil up, simmer for half an hour, then strain. Reserve the liquid.
2. Poach the hake cutlets in the court bouillon for about 10 minutes. Lift out and keep warm.
3. To make the sauce, melt the butter and when melted add the cornflour, mixing quickly.
4. Heat to thicken slightly, stirring all the time, then add the lemon juice and mix well.
5. Season to taste.
6. Serve the sauce with the hake, pouring a little of it over before serving. Garnish with a lemon twist and a sprig of fennel.

BUTTERED CRAB

450 g (1 lb) fresh or frozen crab meat
2 anchovy fillets
150 ml (¼ pint) dry white wine
pinch of grated nutmeg or mace
4 tablespoons fresh white breadcrumbs
salt
freshly ground black pepper
75 g (3 oz) butter
4 slices hot crustless buttered toast

Preparation time: 15 minutes
Cooking time: 15 minutes

1. Flake the crab meat coarsely.
2. Pound up the anchovies in the wine, add the nutmeg, breadcrumbs and seasonings. Put into a saucepan and bring gently to the boil, then simmer for about 3 minutes.
3. Mix the flaked crab meat with the butter and add to the hot wine mixture, stir and cook gently for 4 minutes.
4. Have the hot buttered toast ready. Serve the crab on top of it, or cut the toast into fingers and arrange the fingers of toast around the dish.

HERRINGS MARINATED AND BAKED IN TEA

This is an excellent West Country method of pickling fish. Mackerel, sprats or pilchards can be cooked in this way.

8 herrings, cleaned
8 bay leaves
1 tablespoon brown sugar
15 whole black peppercorns
150 ml ($\frac{1}{4}$ pint) white vinegar
150 ml ($\frac{1}{4}$ pint) cold, milkless tea

Preparation time: 30 minutes
Cooking time: approximately 1 hour
Oven: 180°C, 350°F, Gas Mark 4

1. Lay the fish in an ovenproof dish and put a bay leaf, crumbled, into each one. Sprinkle evenly with the brown sugar and peppercorns.
2. Combine the vinegar and tea, then pour the mixture over the fish so that they are barely covered.
3. Cover loosely with foil and bake in the preheated oven for about 1 hour.
4. Leave to get cold in the liquor, which will jell slightly. Serve a little of the jelly with each portion.

From the left: *Hake with lemon butter sauce, Buttered crab, Herrings marinated and baked in tea*

From the top, clockwise: *Ham with raisin and celery sauce, Beef braised with beer and Cheddar cheese dumplings, Lamb roasted and stuffed with apples and cider*

LAMB ROASTED AND STUFFED WITH APPLES AND CIDER

Serves 6–8
1·75 kg (4 lb) loin of lamb, boned
1 tablespoon lemon juice
grated rind of 1 lemon
450 g (1 lb) cooking apples, peeled, cored and sliced
2 tablespoons brown sugar
½ teaspoon ground cloves
2 tablespoons oil
2 teaspoons ground ginger
salt
freshly ground black pepper
600 ml (1 pint) dry cider or apple juice

Preparation time: 30 minutes
Cooking time: 2 hours
Oven: 200°C, 400°F, Gas Mark 6
then: 180°C, 350°F, Gas Mark 4

1. Lay the boned lamb on a board, then rub it inside and out with the lemon juice and scatter over the rind.
2. Lay the slices of apples inside the meat, sprinkle with sugar and cloves, then roll up, skewering or tying securely.
3. Rub all over the outside with the oil, then the ginger, salt and pepper.
4. Put into the roasting pan and roast in the preheated oven for 30 minutes, then reduce the oven temperature. If you like meat which will be slightly pink in the centre, cook for 20 minutes per 450 g (1 lb); allow 30 minutes per 450 g (1 lb) for well-done meat.
5. Meanwhile warm up the cider and baste the meat with it about every 20 minutes.
6. When the meat is cooked lift it on to a warmed serving dish and keep warm.
7. Skim or pour off any excess fat from the roasting pan, then put it over a hot flame to reduce the cooking liquid slightly until it is a little syrupy. Taste for seasoning and serve the sauce separately.

HAM WITH RAISIN AND CELERY SAUCE

For this recipe, the ham can simply be boiled and served with the sauce, or it can be baked as well.

Serves 6–8
1.75 kg (4 lb) joint of ham or shoulder of bacon,
soaked overnight
600 ml (1 pint) dry cider
1 large onion, peeled and stuck with cloves
sprig of parsley
1 teaspoon brown sugar
freshly ground black pepper
½ lemon
Baked ham (optional):
3–4 tablespoons breadcrumbs
2 tablespoons soft brown sugar
½ teaspoon ground nutmeg or mace
1 tablespoon made English mustard
1–2 tablespoons ham stock
Sauce:
1 rounded tablespoon butter
1 rounded tablespoon flour
300 ml (½ pint) ham stock, hot
4 tablespoons dry cider
50 g (2 oz) raisins or sultanas
2 celery sticks, finely chopped
pinch of nutmeg
2 tablespoons single cream

Preparation time: 15 minutes, plus soaking
overnight
Cooking time: 2–2½ hours
Oven: 200°C, 400°F, Gas Mark 6

1. Drain the ham and scrape the outer skin. Put into a large saucepan with enough cider barely to cover it, together with the onion, parsley, sugar, pepper and lemon.
2. Bring to the boil, skimming if necessary, then simmer gently for 25 minutes per 450 g (1 lb).
3. Leave to cool in the saucepan, then lift out on to a plate and peel off the skin. Reserve the stock.
4. For baked ham, mix together the bread-crumbs, sugar and nutmeg or mace and mustard. Moisten with ham stock and mix to a paste.
5. Press this mixture over the fat top of the ham and lift into an ovenproof dish. Pour around 300 ml (½ pint) of the stock and bake in the preheated oven for 30–40 minutes or until the topping is crisp and brown. Serve hot or cold.
6. To make the sauce, heat the butter and when foaming stir in the flour, then cook for 1 minute.
7. Gradually add the hot stock, stirring well. When it is smooth add the dry cider and stir again.
8. Add the raisins, chopped celery and nutmeg and cook for 4–5 minutes. Finally add the cream. Reheat but do not reboil.

BEEF BRAISED WITH BEER AND CHEDDAR CHEESE DUMPLINGS

A delicious and economical meal using good West Country ingredients. Dumplings are known as 'doughboys' in the West Country.

25 g (1 oz) beef dripping or oil
2 medium onions, peeled and sliced
750 g (1½ lb) stewing beef, cubed
1 rounded tablespoon plain flour
1 teaspoon brown sugar
1 pinch of cinnamon
300 ml (½ pint) brown ale
salt
freshly ground black pepper
Dumplings:
100 g (4 oz) self-raising flour
50 g (2 oz) shredded suet or melted margarine
25 g (1 oz) Cheddar cheese, grated
salt
freshly ground black pepper
2–3 tablespoons water

Preparation time: 30 minutes
Cooking time: about 2 hours
Oven: 180°C, 350°F, Gas Mark 4
then: 160°C, 325°F, Gas Mark 3

1. Heat the fat or oil and soften the onions, then take them out and put into a casserole.
2. Quickly brown the beef on all sides, then add the flour and let it cook for 1 minute, stirring from time to time.
3. Add the sugar and cinnamon and gradually pour in the brown ale. Stir well, then add salt and pepper to taste.
4. Put the meat and gravy into the casserole, cover and cook in the preheated oven for half an hour, then reduce the oven temperature and continue cooking for a further hour.
5. For the dumplings, mix together all the dry ingredients. Add the water gradually, adding a little more if needed to make a fairly slack dough.
6. Flour the hands and break the dough into 8 small pieces, then roll into little balls with the palms of the hands. Chill until required.
7. After 1½ hours' cooking time, test the meat with a fork. If necessary, cook for a further half an hour. If the casserole seems dry, add a little water, or more beer.
8. About 20 minutes before the meat is ready, place the dumplings on top of the casserole, leave off the lid and cook until they are risen, about 20–30 minutes.
9. Alternatively, poach the dumplings, about 4 at a time, in a saucepan of boiling salted water, for about 15 minutes. Drain well.

APPLE PIE WITH ALMOND PASTRY

The pie is eaten warm with clotted cream. It can either be made in a shallow dish with a double crust, as described here, or in a deeper dish with a single crust.

Serves 4–6

Pastry:
175 g (6 oz) plain flour
2 rounded tablespoons ground almonds
100 g (4 oz) butter, warm
25 g (1 oz) icing sugar
1 egg yolk
2 tablespoons cold water
a little milk for glazing
Filling:
750 g (1½ lb) apples, peeled, cored and sliced, or
450 g (1 lb) apples and 225 g (½ lb) blackberries
2 teaspoons lemon juice
100 g (4 oz) caster sugar

Preparation time: 50 minutes
Cooking time: 40 minutes
Oven: 200°C, 400°F, Gas Mark 6
then: 160°C, 325°F, Gas Mark 3

From the left: *Fairings, Apple pie with almond pastry*

1. First make the pastry by putting the flour and almonds into the basin, then add the butter, at room temperature. Cut into small pieces and rub into the flour.
2. Add the sifted icing sugar, mixing well.
3. Make a well in the centre and put the egg yolk and water mixed together into it. Mix to a rough dough in the basin with a fork.
4. Turn on to a lightly floured surface and knead gently until it is quite smooth. Roll into a ball and chill for at least 30 minutes before using.
5. If using blackberries, put them into a dish and place in the oven while it is heating up.
6. Divide the pastry into 2 and roll out to fit a 20 cm (8 inch) shallow pie plate and line it with one half of the pastry. Fill the pie with the apples (or blackberries and apples), the lemon juice, about 3–4 tablespoons of blackberry juice, if using, from the warmed dish, and the sugar.
7. Dampen the edges and lay the other piece of pastry on top, pressing down the edges with finger and thumb.
8. Make a small slit in the middle to let the air out, or prick lightly all over the top, and brush with a little milk.
9. Bake in the centre of the preheated oven for 20 minutes, then reduce the oven temperature for a further 15–20 minutes. Serve warm with clotted cream.

FAIRINGS

These are little biscuits sold at the fairs which were held all over the West Country. There are several kinds but these are the crunchy Cornish variety.

Makes about 30 biscuits
225 g (8 oz) self-raising flour
1½ teaspoons bicarbonate of soda
pinch of salt
1 teaspoon ground ginger
1 teaspoon mixed spice
½ teaspoon ground cinnamon
100 g (4 oz) butter or margarine
50 g (2 oz) sugar
100 g (4 oz) golden syrup

Preparation time: 25 minutes
Cooking time: about 10 minutes
Oven: 190°C, 375°F, Gas Mark 5

1. Sift the flour, bicarbonate of soda, salt and spices together and mix well.
2. Then rub in the butter and add the sugar so the mixture looks like breadcrumbs.
3. Heat the golden syrup a little, then pour it into the paste and knead until it forms a firm dough.
4. Flour your hands and roll the mixture into small balls, then put on to a greased baking sheet, well spaced out. Flatten down well with the back of a spoon.
5. Cook in the centre of the preheated oven for about 10 minutes or until golden brown. Remove from the baking sheet and cool on a wire tray.

DEVONSHIRE SPLITS

These yeasted buns form the basis of many 'Cream Teas' in Devon and Cornwall. They are split open and served with clotted cream and strawberry or raspberry jam. If served with clotted cream and black treacle they are known as 'Thunder and Lightning'.

Makes about 18 buns
15 g (½ oz) fresh yeast or 10 g (¼ oz) dried yeast
¼ teaspoon caster sugar
150 ml (¼ pint) tepid water
25 g (1 oz) lard
50 g (2 oz) butter
6 tablespoons milk
450 g (1 lb) plain flour
pinch of salt
icing sugar
clotted cream or whipped cream
jam

Preparation time: 15 minutes, plus rising
Cooking time: 20 minutes
Oven: 200°C, 400°F, Gas Mark 6

Devonshire splits

1. Sprinkle the yeast and sugar over the tepid water and leave until it is frothy. If using dried yeast, mix with the sugar and tepid water and leave in a warm place for about 10 minutes, until it becomes frothy.
2. Put the lard, butter and milk into a small saucepan and heat gently until the fats have melted, but on no account let it boil. Remove from the heat and allow to cool.
3. Meanwhile sift the flour and salt into a mixing bowl, make a well in the centre and pour in the yeast and milk mixtures, then mix with the fingers until it is soft but not sticky.
4. Turn on to a floured surface and knead gently for 5 minutes, then put into a bowl and leave covered in a warm place for 1 hour.
5. Take out and knead again a little, then shape into about 18 small balls. Place them on a greased baking sheet a little apart and leave until they have spread and are just touching.
6. Bake in the preheated oven for about 20 minutes or until risen. When cooked, they should sound hollow when tapped. Dust with icing sugar, and serve with clotted cream and jam.

SAFFRON CAKE

Saffron is derived from the dried and powdered stigmas and parts of the styles of the saffron crocus (*crocus sativus*) which should not be confused with the autumn crocus which it resembles. As it requires many thousands of crocus flowers to make even small quantities of saffron it is easy to see why it is so expensive today. It was introduced into Cornwall by the Phoenicians at a very early date when they first came to England to trade for tin. It still forms a part of the flavouring for a traditional cake or loaf in Cornwall, imparting a honey-like taste and a glorious golden colour.

Serves 6–8
$\frac{1}{2}$ teaspoon saffron strands
300 ml ($\frac{1}{2}$ pint) hot milk
15 g ($\frac{1}{2}$ oz) fresh yeast or 10 g ($\frac{1}{4}$ oz) dried yeast
25 g (1 oz) caster sugar
450 g (1 lb) strong plain flour
100 g (4 oz) butter
150 g (5 oz) currants
50 g (2 oz) chopped, mixed candied peel

Preparation time: 45 minutes, plus 1$\frac{1}{4}$ hours soaking
Cooking time: 1 hour
Oven: 200°C, 400°F, Gas Mark 6, then 180°C, 350°F, Gas Mark 4

1. Infuse the saffron strands in the hot milk and leave for at least 1 hour, then strain and heat the liquid to tepid.
2. Cream the yeast with 1 teaspoon of the sugar, leave until it begins to foam a little, then gradually add the tepid saffron milk. If using dried yeast, mix with half the milk and the sugar and leave in a warm place for about 10 minutes, until it becomes frothy, then add the rest of the milk.
3. Reserve 1 teaspoon of flour, then sift the remainder into a mixing bowl. Cut the butter into small pieces, and rub in to the flour.
4. Make a well in the middle and pour in the yeast liquid. Sprinkle the reserved flour over the top of the yeast liquid and leave to stand in a warm place for 15–20 minutes until it froths up.
5. Add the currants, candied peel and the remaining sugar. Mix to a soft dough, beating well. When the dough becomes shiny and elastic turn into a 20 cm (8 inch) greased cake tin and cover with a damp cloth. Leave in a warm place until double in size.
6. Bake in the centre of the preheated oven for 30 minutes, then reduce the temperature and bake for another 30 minutes. Do not open the oven door while the mixture is cooking. Leave to cool in the tin, then turn out.
7. Serve cut into slices with clotted cream or butter. When stale it is very good toasted.

DAMASK CREAM

This is an old recipe for junket which was popular in eighteenth-century Bath. In Devon and Cornwall it is served with clotted cream on top.

600 ml (1 pint) single cream
2 rounded tablespoons caster sugar
2 teaspoons rennet or junket tablets
pinch of grated nutmeg
4 tablespoons double or whipping cream
3 tablespoons rosewater (obtainable at chemist shops)
1 tablespoon sugar
To decorate:
deep red rose petals, if liked

Preparation time: 15 minutes, plus setting
Cooking time: 5 minutes

1. Make the junket by heating the single cream to no higher than tepid (36.9°C/98.4°F). Add the sugar, stirring to dissolve it, then stir in either the rennet or the junket tablets. Mix well and pour into a serving dish.
2. Leave to set for about 2 hours. Do not move or otherwise disturb while it is clotting.
3. When the junket is set, sprinkle with a little grated nutmeg.
4. About 30 minutes before serving, mix together the 4 tablespoons cream, the rosewater and sugar and pour this mixture over the top. Serve surrounded by deep red rose petals, if liked.

BATH BUNS

Bath buns are thought to have been the invention of Dr. Oliver of Bath, who was also responsible for the excellent plain biscuit called the Bath Oliver. Bath buns are light and sugary and the most elegant place to eat them is the Pump Room in Bath.

Makes about 10 buns
15 g ($\frac{1}{2}$ oz) fresh yeast or 10 g ($\frac{1}{4}$ oz) dried yeast
1 teaspoon sugar
300 ml ($\frac{1}{2}$ pint) tepid milk
350 g (12 oz) plain flour
100 g (4 oz) butter
75 g (3 oz) caster sugar
2 eggs, beaten
50 g (2 oz) candied peel, chopped
50 g (2 oz) lump sugar, crushed

Preparation time: 10 minutes, plus rising
Cooking time: 30 minutes
Oven: 180°C, 350°F, Gas Mark 4

1. Cream the yeast with the sugar and add to the tepid milk. (If using dried yeast, mix with the sugar and half the milk. Leave in a warm place until frothy, then add the rest of the milk.) Put the flour in a bowl and pour the yeast mixture into a well in the middle. Leave until frothy.
2. Cream the butter and sugar, add the egg, reserving a little to glaze, and work into the dough.
3. Reserve a little peel for decoration, then add the rest to the dough.

4. Cover the dough with a cloth and leave in a warm place to rise for about 40 minutes.
5. Turn out and knead, then shape into buns about 5–7.5 cm (2–3 inches) across and place on a greased baking sheet well spaced out.
6. Leave to rise for a further 15–20 minutes, then brush with the rest of the egg, sprinkle with the coarsely crushed sugar and a little chopped peel.
7. Bake in the preheated oven for about 30 minutes.

From the top, clockwise: *Damask cream, Bath buns, Saffron cake*

SOMERSET STRAWBERRY SHORTCAKE

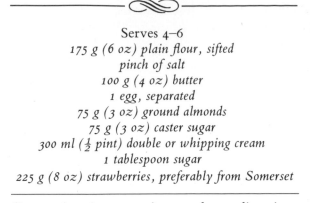

Serves 4–6
175 g (6 oz) plain flour, sifted
pinch of salt
100 g (4 oz) butter
1 egg, separated
75 g (3 oz) ground almonds
75 g (3 oz) caster sugar
300 ml (½ pint) double or whipping cream
1 tablespoon sugar
225 g (8 oz) strawberries, preferably from Somerset

Preparation time: 25 minutes, plus cooling time
Cooking time: 30 minutes
Oven: 160°C, 325°F, Gas Mark 3

1. Sift the flour and salt and rub in the butter.
2. Add the egg yolk, almonds and sugar and mix well.
3. Divide this mixture between 2 × 15 cm (6 inch) greased and lined sandwich tins. Prick the top slightly and bake in the preheated oven for about 30 minutes, or until it starts to shrink away from the sides.
4. Turn out on to a wire rack to cool.
5. About 2 hours before you want to serve the shortcake, whip the cream and sugar to taste. Whip the egg white and add it to the cream.
6. Reserve half the strawberries. Cut the rest into halves or quarters and mix with half the whipped cream.
7. Spread the strawberries and cream mixture on to 1 shortcake. Place the other one on top to form a sandwich.
8. Just before serving, decorate the top with the rest of the whipped cream and the remaining whole strawberries. Do not do this too far in advance or it will make the shortcake soft.

CORNISH BURNT CREAM

Serves 6
6 egg yolks
1 level tablespoon caster sugar
600 ml (1 pint) double or whipping cream
1 vanilla pod
3 tablespoons caster sugar for topping

Preparation time: 25 minutes, plus cooling overnight
Cooking time: 10–15 minutes

1. Mix the beaten egg yolks with the tablespoon of sugar.

2. Put the cream with the vanilla pod in the top of a double saucepan.
3. Bring to scalding point, but do not let it boil. Lift out the vanilla pod with kitchen tongs and pour the hot cream at once on to the egg yolks, whisking continuously until they are well amalgamated.
4. Put the mixture back over a gentle heat, stirring continuously until it thickens slightly so that it runs off the whisk in ribbons. On no account let it boil.
5. Strain into a shallow flameproof dish and leave undisturbed, covered, in a cool place for 6–8 hours, or overnight.
6. Two or three hours before serving, dust the top evenly with the caster sugar, but do not let it become too thick.
7. Put under a preheated grill and, watching it all the time, colour the cream evenly, turning the dish round if necessary until the sugar melts to a golden colour.
8. Remove from the heat and leave in a cool place until needed.

DORSET APPLE CAKE

You can add 2 tablespoons of dried fruit to this Wessex recipe if you prefer.

Serves 6
225 g (8 oz) self-raising flour
pinch of salt
pinch of mixed spice
100 g (4 oz) butter or margarine
100 g (4 oz) soft brown sugar
350 g (12 oz) cooking apples, peeled, cored and finely chopped
1½–2½ tablespoons milk

Preparation time: 20 minutes
Cooking time: 45 minutes–1 hour
Oven: 180°C, 350°F, Gas Mark 4

1. Sift the flour, salt and mixed spice into a bowl and rub in the fat.
2. Mix the sugar with the finely chopped apples and stir into the flour mixture, adding enough milk to form a soft but not sticky dough.
3. Press the dough into a 23 cm (9 inch) flan case placed on a baking sheet.
4. Bake in the preheated oven for about 45–60 minutes or until it is firm when pressed.
5. Serve while still hot and spread with butter on top.

From the top: *Dorset apple cake, Cornish burnt cream, Somerset strawberry shortcake*

LONDON

Since Roman times, London has been a place of importance and for most of that time it has had a reputation for good eating. Moreover, because it has provided a home for many different nationalities, the food available is tremendously varied. Many of these foreign communities kept up their own traditions, which included their original eating habits, and a great number still survive today in parts of London such as the East End, Dockland and Soho.

Highly skilled chefs, employed in hotels, clubs and private houses, transformed this varied produce into wonderful dishes which still survive. John Farley was the principal cook at the famous London Tavern in the 18th century. This tavern served true English food: wonderful meat pies and puddings, huge joints of roast beef, thick chops and steaks and many other well-cooked foods. The Tavern was much admired by the French and the first public restaurant in Paris, which opened in 1782 was called the 'Grande Taverne de Londres', and specialised in such dishes as 'le rosbif, plumbuting and woueche rabette'. High praise indeed!

The elegant homes of the gentry were often crowded, so the men escaped to their clubs around St. James's where they ate very well, or to supper rooms such as the Albion near Drury Lane, or Evans' Supper Rooms. Few places admitted women except hotels and tea rooms. The poorer classes enjoyed their days out on Hampstead Heath, Greenwich or Chelsea where they consumed large quantities of meat pies, jellied eels, muffins, and buns such as the large, curranty Chelsea buns. Inns, too, catered for the crowds with roast joints, chops, steaks and vast steak and kidney puddings, such as is still served at the Cheshire Cheese Tavern in Fleet Street. Many working men and women lived in bed-sitting rooms without cooking facilities, so they enjoyed the good pies, muffins from the muffin man and oysters or eels from the stalls, set around the streets of London. It was good food, ready to eat, an earlier version of the modern takeaway.

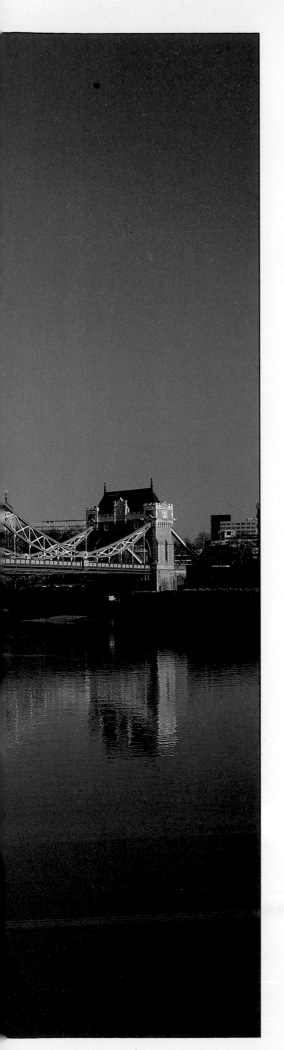

Tower Bridge, London

THE LONDON PARTICULAR

This soup is so-called after the dense London fogs of the last century, generally called 'pea soupers'. One such fog was referred to by a character in Charles Dickens' *Bleak House* as 'a London Particular'.

Serves 6–8

450 g (1 lb) green split peas, soaked
4 rashers bacon, diced or a meaty ham-bone
1 large onion, sliced
2.4 litres (4 pints) water, or stock from boiled ham or bacon, not too salty
freshly ground black pepper
2 teaspoons Worcestershire sauce
3 tablespoons single cream (optional)
To garnish:
small croûtons of fried bread

Preparation time: 10 minutes, plus soaking time
Cooking time: 2 hours

1. Soak the dried split peas in enough cold water to cover for at least 4 hours, preferably overnight.
2. Cook the bacon in a large saucepan until the fat runs out, then just soften the onion in the fat.
3. Add the peas, the soaking liquid and the water or stock; cover and bring to the boil.
4. Skin off any scum if necessary, then lower the heat and simmer for about 2 hours, stirring from time to time to prevent sticking. The peas will be almost puréed by then.
5. Stir well and taste for seasoning, then add the Worcestershire sauce.
6. Before serving stir in the cream, if liked, or float it on top.
7. Serve garnished with small croûtons.

CELERY SOUP

Celery soup was very popular in many London clubs and restaurants. Good celery was brought to the London markets, the hearts being served with cheese and the rest being made into soups or used, cooked, as a vegetable.

Serves 6

1 large head of celery, washed and trimmed
1 medium onion, sliced
300 ml ($\frac{1}{2}$ pint) chicken stock
600 ml (1 pint) milk
1 tablespoon plain flour
1 tablespoon butter
300 ml ($\frac{1}{2}$ pint) single cream
salt
freshly ground black pepper
pinch of nutmeg

Preparation time: 30 minutes
Cooking time: 2 hours

1. Chop the celery into small pieces, removing any strings from the outer stalks. Put it into a large saucepan with the onion and stock; bring to the boil and simmer for 30 minutes.
2. Add the milk, bring back to the boil, then simmer until it is tender, for about 40–60 minutes.
3. Take off, cool a little, then sieve or blend until it is very smooth.
4. Blend the flour and the butter into a firm paste.
5. Return the soup to the heat and drop small pieces of the butter paste into it, stirring all the time. Simmer gently until the soup has thickened slightly.
6. Remove from the heat and add the cream, salt, pepper and nutmeg.
7. Reheat gently, but do not boil.

OMELETTE ARNOLD BENNETT

The chef of the Savoy Hotel created this late supper dish for the writer Arnold Bennett when he worked as a theatre critic.

Serves 2

275 g (10 oz) smoked haddock, cooked, skinned and flaked
2 tablespoons grated Parmesan cheese
freshly ground black pepper
1 heaped teaspoon butter
6 eggs (size 1), lightly beaten
3–4 tablespoons thick double or whipping cream

Preparation time: 30 minutes
Cooking time: 7 minutes

1. Mix the smoked haddock with the Parmesan cheese. Add pepper to taste.
2. Melt the butter in a heavy frying or omelette pan and swirl the pan until it is completely coated with butter. Do not let the butter brown.
3. Pour in the eggs which should sizzle slightly, then at once, with either a spatula or small slice, move the eggs into the middle but tip the pan so that the uncooked egg which is left runs over and covers the bottom.
4. When the bottom is just set but the top is still creamy and liquid spoon on the fish and cheese mixture evenly. Pour the thick cream smoothly on top.
5. Heat the grill. Remove the omelette pan from the heat, sprinkle the top with freshly ground pepper and put under the hot grill until it is puffed up and golden.
6. Do not attempt to fold this omelette; simply slide it off the pan, cream side up, on to a hot plate.

POTTED CHEESE

Potted cheese was a favourite first course. Sometimes it was also served as a last course or a snack meal, with pickled onions or celery and beer. Potted cheese will keep for several weeks in a cool place so long as the butter seal is not broken.

Serves 8–10

450 g (1 lb) hard cheese such as Cheddar, grated
1 teaspoon dry mustard powder
½ teaspoon powdered mace
¼ teaspoon cayenne pepper
175 g (6 oz) butter
150 ml (¼ pint) sweet sherry or sweet white wine
3 tablespoons melted butter

Preparation time: 25 minutes

1. Pound up all the dry ingredients with the butter to a smooth paste. This can be done in a food processor or by hand.
2. Add the wine gradually, mixing each time until it is quite absorbed before adding more.
3. When the cheese mixture is creamy and smooth, put into either one large pot or several smaller ones, pressing it down firmly to avoid air bubbles.
4. Pour the melted butter gently over the top or tops. Leave undisturbed until it has set.
5. Serve like a pâté with hot toast.

FRIED WHITEBAIT

From medieval times it was a summer custom to travel down the Thames from Westminster Bridge to Greenwich, there to consume freshly caught whitebait at various pubs and hotels.

150 g (5 oz) seasoned flour
900 g (2 lb) fresh whitebait, washed and thoroughly dried
oil for deep frying
salt
freshly ground black pepper
lemon wedges

Preparation time: 15 minutes
Cooking time: 5–7 minutes

1. Put about half the flour into a large plastic bag with a large handful of whitebait. Shake them around until they are well coated with flour. Continue until all the whitebait are coated.
2. Heat the oil in a deep fryer to 180°–190°C/350°–375°F or until a cube of bread browns in 30 seconds. Deep-fry the whitebait in batches for 2–3 minutes. When golden all over, lift out and drain on paper towels.
3. Keep the whitebait in a warm place until they are all ready, then return to the pan and deep-fry again for about 1 minute.
4. Serve at once with salt, pepper, lemon wedges and brown bread and butter.

From the top, clockwise: *Celery soup, Potted cheese, Omelette Arnold Bennett*

STEAK, KIDNEY AND OYSTER PUDDING

Steak, kidney and oyster pudding is one of the glories of English cooking. It has been made for many centuries and was the speciality of many taverns in London, particularly the Cheshire Cheese in Fleet Street, where it is still served.

Serves 6–8
225 g (8 oz) shredded suet
450 g (1 lb) plain flour
50 g (2 oz) fresh white breadcrumbs
pinch of salt
300 ml (½ pint) cold water
Filling:
2 tablespoons plain flour, seasoned
1.4 kg (3 lb) rump steak trimmed and cut into 2.5 cm (1 inch) cubes
450 g (1 lb) ox kidney, chopped
1 small onion, grated
salt
freshly ground black pepper
2 teaspoons Worcestershire sauce
2 teaspoons chopped parsley
6 oysters, fresh or canned
600 ml (1 pint) beef stock

Preparation time: 45 minutes
Cooking time: 5 hours

1. Lightly grease a 2.3 litre (4 pint) pudding basin.
2. Mix together all the dry ingredients, then add the water slowly, mixing to make a smooth pliable dough.
3. Turn on to a floured surface and roll out. Reserve enough to cover the top. Cut a strip long enough to line the basin sides, plus a round for the bottom. Press to seal the edges.
4. Sift the flour on to a flat plate, then roll the meat and onion in it and put into the lined basin.
5. Add salt, pepper, Worcestershire sauce, the parsley and oysters, and mix in carefully.
6. Add the stock, which should not come higher than 1 cm (½ inch) from the top.
7. Roll out the remaining suet crust to fit the top. Dampen the edge and lay it on, pressing down at the rim.
8. Cover with buttered greaseproof paper or foil which is pleated across the middle to allow the pudding to rise. Tie securely and stand in the top of a steamer or else in a deep saucepan.
9. Pour in boiling water. If the pudding is in a saucepan, do not let the water come above the rim of the basin. Put the lid on the saucepan or steamer and cook for 4–5 hours, topping up the water as necessary. Longer cooking will only improve the pudding.
10. To serve, remove the paper or foil and wrap the basin in a napkin or folded teatowel.

STUFFED SHOULDER OF LAMB WITH ONION SAUCE

Serves 6–8
1 shoulder of lamb, about 2 kg (4 lb), boned and trimmed
freshly ground black pepper
2 tablespoons dripping or oil
1 teaspoon seasoned plain flour
Stuffing:
4 tablespoons fresh breadcrumbs
2 tablespoons milk
2 rashers bacon, chopped
2 shallots or small onions, chopped
½ teaspoon rosemary
¼ teaspoon parsley
grated rind of ½ lemon
1 teaspoon lemon juice
salt
freshly ground black pepper
Sauce:
2 tablespoons butter
3 large onions, peeled and finely sliced
1 heaped tablespoon plain flour
300 ml (½ pint) milk
pinch of nutmeg
salt
freshly ground black pepper
150 ml (¼ pint) cream

Preparation time: 30 minutes
Cooking time: 2 hours
Oven: 190°C, 375°F, Gas Mark 5

1. Lay the meat on a board and open it out, skin side downwards. Season with black pepper.
2. Make the stuffing by combining all the ingredients and mixing well. Spread it over the meat.
3. Roll up the meat securely and fasten with small skewers or sew it up.
4. Put into the roasting tin, dust the outside with pepper and add the dripping or oil.
5. Cook in the preheated oven for 20 minutes per 450 g (1 lb).
6. Half-way through the cooking time, strain off any excess fat. Baste from time to time.
7. Heat the butter until it foams, then just soften the onions in it, but do not colour. Sprinkle the flour over and cook for 1 minute.
8. Add the milk slowly, stirring to avoid lumps, add nutmeg and season to taste. Simmer until the sauce is smooth and creamy, then remove from the heat.
9. About 15 minutes before the joint is ready, take it out, shake over the seasoned flour, and sprinkle over a few drops of cold water. Return to the oven to let the top crisp.
10. Place the joint on a warm serving dish.
11. Stir the cream into the onion sauce and gently reheat. Serve in a gravy boat.

From the top: *Steak, kidney and oyster pudding, Stuffed shoulder of lamb with onion sauce, Fried whitebait (page 121), The London particular (page 120)*

PORK PIE

Meat pies of many descriptions are particularly associated with London. Pork pies are perhaps the most popular, followed by veal and ham or beef pies, but mutton and rabbit can also be made in the same way. In his book *London Labour and the London Poor*, Mayhew said the itinerant trade in pies still in evidence at the end of the nineteenth century was one of the most ancient of the street callings of London.

Serves 4–6
Jellied stock:
pork bones (ask the butcher for these)
2 pig's trotters
1 large carrot, scraped and sliced
1 medium onion, peeled and sliced
pinch of mixed herbs
10 whole black peppercorns
3 litres (5 pints) water
Hot-water crust:
200 ml ($\frac{1}{3}$ pint) water
175 g (6 oz) lard
450 g (1 lb) plain flour
$\frac{1}{2}$ teaspoon salt
1 egg (optional)
Glaze:
beaten egg
Filling:
1 kg (2$\frac{1}{4}$ lb) boned pork shoulder, finely chopped
225 g (8 oz) thinly sliced unsmoked bacon rashers, chopped
$\frac{1}{2}$ teaspoon dried sage
$\frac{1}{2}$ teaspoon ground cinnamon
$\frac{1}{2}$ teaspoon ground nutmeg
$\frac{1}{2}$ teaspoon ground allspice
1 teaspoon anchovy essence
salt
freshly ground black pepper

Preparation time: 1 hour
Cooking time: 5 hours
Oven 200°C, 400°F, Gas Mark 6
then: 160°C, 325°F, Gas Mark 3

1. First make the stock. Put all the ingredients in a large saucepan, bring to the boil and skim off any foam or scum. Simmer steadily for 2 hours, then strain, cool and skim off the fat.
2. Bring the water and lard to the boil and have the flour and salt ready in a bowl nearby. When the liquid boils tip it quickly into the flour and mix rapidly together to a smooth dough.
3. Add the egg if using; it gives good colour and extra richness but is not essential.
4. Leave the dough, covered, in a warm place until it cools just enough to handle it easily, but do not let it get cold or it will disintegrate.
5. Turn the dough on to a floured surface. Reserve enough for a lid, then put the remainder into a hinged pie mould or an 18 cm (7 inch) round cake tin with a removable base.
6. Quickly and lightly push the pastry up the sides of the tin, leaving no cracks. If it collapses, wait a little and try again, or roll it out. Set aside.
7. Mix together all the ingredients for the filling.
8. Pack the filling into the pastry case, letting it mound up over the rim a little.
9. Roll out the lid, brush the edges with beaten egg and press it on.
10. Make a central hole and roll out a small leaf or rose to cover this.
11. Brush over with the beaten egg and bake in the preheated oven for 30 minutes.
12. Reduce the oven temperature and leave for a further 1$\frac{1}{2}$–2 hours, to allow the meat to cook. Cover with foil if it browns too quickly.
13. Take the pie from the oven, cool for 30 minutes, then turn it out of the mould or tin.
14. Brush the sides with beaten egg and put back in the oven for about 10 minutes to colour.
15. When the pie crust is lightly browned all over, remove from the oven, lift off the rose and, with a small funnel, pour in some of the stock which will turn to jelly when cold.
16. Leave the pie for 24 hours in a cool place before eating.

From the bottom, clockwise: *York Club cutlets, Lord Mayor's trifle (page 126), Pork pie*

YORK CLUB CUTLETS

The fashionable London clubs of the seventeenth and eighteenth centuries employed excellent chefs who produced many original dishes.

---

4 thick lamb chump chops
freshly ground black pepper
1 rounded tablespoon breadcrumbs
1 rounded teaspoon butter
Sauce:
4 medium onions, peeled and sliced
50 g (2 oz) butter
1 teaspoon sugar
1 rounded tablespoon plain flour
150 ml ($\frac{1}{4}$ pint) onion stock, warm
300 ml ($\frac{1}{2}$ pint) milk
salt
pepper
2 tablespoons cream

Preparation time: 30 minutes
Cooking time: 50 minutes
Oven: 200°C, 400°F, Gas Mark 6

---

1. First make enough sauce by boiling the sliced onions in water to cover for 10 minutes. Strain and reserve the liquid.
2. Heat the butter, add the onions and the sugar, and fry until they are a soft purée.
3. Stir in the flour, mixing well, and let it cook for 1 minute, then add the warm onion stock, stirring all the time until it thickens and is smooth.
4. Then stir in the milk, bring to boiling point, stirring all the time until it is smooth and creamy.
5. Season to taste and finally add the cream. Keep warm, but do not let it boil.
6. Trim the chops and dust with black pepper. Grill them lightly on one side only.
7. Put them cooked side down in a baking dish, then cover with the onion sauce.
8. Sprinkle the breadcrumbs all over and put a nut of butter on each cutlet.
9. Put into the preheated oven fairly near the top and cook for about 15–20 minutes, depending on whether you like well-cooked or medium-cooked meat. The top should be gently browned and crisp.

Variation: If preferred, the cutlets can be grilled on both sides in the usual way and the sauce served with them. However the crisp crust is extremely good.

RICHMOND MAIDS OF HONOUR

These cakes are reputed to have been made first at the court of Henry VIII. There is a cake shop in Richmond where they are still sold.

Makes 20 cakes
225 g (8 oz) puff pastry
225 g (8 oz) ground almonds
100 g (4 oz) caster sugar
2 eggs, beaten
25 g (1 oz) plain flour
4 tablespoons single cream
2 teaspoons lemon juice

Preparation time: 45 minutes
Cooking time: 15 minutes
Oven: 200°C, 400°F, Gas Mark 6

1. Roll out the pastry on a lightly floured surface and cut out rounds for 20 × 8 cm (3 inch) patty tins.
2. Mix together the ground almonds and sugar.
3. Add the beaten eggs and mix in the flour, cream and lemon juice.
4. Divide the mixture between the pastry cases and bake for about 15 minutes in the preheated oven, or until firm and golden brown.

1. Put the sifted flour and salt into a warm bowl and stir in half the sugar. Rub in half the butter and make a well in the centre.
2. Sprinkle the yeast and 1 teaspoon sugar over the tepid milk and leave until frothy. If using dried yeast, mix with the sugar and water and leave in a warm place for 10 minutes, until frothy. Add the beaten eggs.
3. Pour the yeast into the flour mixture and mix well. Turn out on to a floured surface and knead lightly until smooth. Put back in the bowl, cover and leave in a warm place until double in size.
4. Soften the remaining butter.
5. Turn out the dough on to a floured surface, knead lightly and roll it into a rectangle about 1 cm (½ inch) thick. Spread with the remaining butter and sprinkle with the remaining sugar. Fold dough in half and roll out again to the same thickness.
6. Scatter over the currants and the spice, then roll up from the long side like a Swiss roll. Cut into 4 cm (1½ inch) slices.
7. Grease the baking sheet, then lay the slices on it, fairly close together, cut sides uppermost. Cover and leave in a warm place for 20 minutes.
8. The buns should now be touching. Put into the preheated oven for about 20 minutes.
9. To make the glaze, boil the sugar and water for 7 minutes. When cooked, brush the buns with the glaze and put back for 5 minutes to dry. Do not separate until cool.

CHELSEA BUNS

The Old Chelsea Bun House in the Pimlico Road sold as many as a quarter of a million buns a day until it was burnt down in 1839. George III and Queen Charlotte were frequent customers and would sit on the verandah munching buns, to the delight of the crowd.

Makes about 12 buns
500 g (1¼ lb) plain flour, sifted and warmed
pinch of salt
150 g (5 oz) caster sugar
150 g (5 oz) butter
25 g (1 oz) fresh yeast or 15 g (½ oz) dried yeast
1 teaspoon sugar
150 ml (¼ pint) tepid milk
4 eggs, beaten
100 g (4 oz) currants
1 teaspoon mixed spice
50 g (2 oz) granulated sugar
2 tablespoons water

Preparation time: 30 minutes, plus proving time
Cooking time: 35 minutes
Oven: 200°C, 400°F, Gas Mark 6

LORD MAYOR'S TRIFLE

Serves 8
6 sponge cakes, about 10 × 5 cm (4 × 2 inches)
24 small ratafia biscuits
8 small almond macaroons
150 ml (¼ pint) brandy or sherry
6 tablespoons strawberry or raspberry jam
300 ml (½ pint) double or whipping cream, whipped
chopped almonds and glacé fruits, to decorate
Custard:
600 ml (1 pint) milk
2 tablespoons caster sugar
4 egg yolks, beaten

Preparation time: 40 minutes, plus soaking
Cooking time: 15 minutes

1. Slice the sponge cakes and put at the bottom of a deep dish. Add the ratafia biscuits and the macaroons, crumbled. Pour over the brandy or sherry and leave, covered, to soak for at least 4 hours.
2. Heat the milk with the sugar until the sugar has dissolved. Pour the milk over the egg yolks, beating all the time.
3. Return to the saucepan, and stir over moderate heat until the liquid will coat the back of a spoon.

Do not allow the custard to boil or it will curdle.
4. Remove from the heat and stir to prevent a skin forming. Allow to cool, covered.
5. Spread the jam over the sponge cakes.
6. Pour the cold custard over the cakes.
7. About 30 minutes before serving, cover the top with the whipped cream piled high, and decorate with the nuts and chopped fruit.

WHIPPED LONDON SYLLABUB

Serves 4–6
1 tablespoon caster sugar
300 ml (½ pint) Madeira wine or Marsala
a good pinch of nutmeg
600 ml (1 pint) double or whipping cream, whipped until stiff

Preparation time: 15 minutes, plus cooling time

1. Mix together the sugar, wine and nutmeg, then divide it between 4 or 6 long narrow glasses.
2. Divide the whipped cream between the glasses, putting it on top of the wine mixture.
3. Leave in a cool place for several hours or overnight before serving.

BOODLE'S ORANGE FOOL

This recipe is from Boodle's Club in St. James's Street, founded in 1763.

Serves 4–6
2 lemons
4 large oranges
2 tablespoons sugar, or to taste
6 sponge cakes, about 10 × 5 cm (4 × 2 inches)
600 ml (1 pint) double or whipping cream

Preparation time: 30 minutes, plus 2–3 hours soaking time

1. Finely grate the rind of the lemons and 2 of the oranges into a bowl, then squeeze the juice from all the fruit.
2. Sweeten with the sugar to taste.
3. Cut the sponge cakes into 4 pieces each and put in the bottom of a serving dish.
4. Pour the cream in a steady stream into the fruit juice and rind, stirring very lightly.
5. Pour this mixture over the cakes and leave for at least 2–3 hours to let the juice and the cream penetrate the sponge cakes.

From the left:
Richmond maids of honour (top), Chelsea buns (bottom), Whipped London syllabub, Boodle's orange fool

The SOUTH

Kent, Sussex and the Home Counties

In the seventeenth century, English landowners began to take an interest in their parks and pleasure gardens as well as in their kitchen gardens. New seeds and varieties of plants were introduced, especially from Holland. As a result of this enthusiasm, nursery gardening, particularly in and around London, became a paying profession. Great lords, whose fathers had hardly known one plant from another, began to observe and examine each others' gardens. Successful head gardeners were in great demand; the best were sometimes tempted away from one estate to another by higher wages and the challenge of improving the gardens. Such gardeners would meet and exchange ideas and seeds with one another and visit the new specialist London nurseries to acquire the fashionable dwarf fruit trees, rare shrubs, lilies and roses. Hot houses became fashionable. Peaches, nectarines and apricots were grown and many a head gardener was ordered to grow pineapples, which always proved difficult. Orangeries were built, ostensibly for growing fruit but really for ornament, as the fruit seldom ripened well.

Since many royal palaces and great estates were built or created in the South, fine food in large quantities was required from the time of Henry VIII, who often resided at Hampton Court (where as many as three thousand were feasted) to that of the lavish Victorian house parties in castles and manor houses, where 20 or 30 guests might be entertained at a seven-course dinner. Farmers were encouraged to breed specially fattened beef and veal. Surrey has for centuries been famous for its chickens and capons, as Buckinghamshire has for its great, white Aylesbury ducks.

Kent, with its splendid cherries, its hops and the fine wheat grown on the Weald, has certain entirely local dishes. The coast produced fine fishing and Whitstable oysters were considered to be as good as those of Colchester. The Lord Warden of the Cinque Ports, who was obliged to give several official dinners a year, traditionally offered one great fish dish. This consisted of the head and shoulders of a large cod, just caught, boiled, partly masked with coral-pink shrimp sauce and surrounded with 'one hundred oysters and as many prawns, with a great wreath of parsley round the edge of the plate and the claw meat of lobsters set in it like pieces of coral'.

In general, the cooking of the South and the Home Counties is, perhaps, the most sophisticated in all England.

Oast houses, Chiddingstone, Kent

CUCUMBER AND STILTON MOUSSE

⁓

This elegant summer dish was served on the Cunard liner, the *Queen Mary*, famous for its lavish cuisine.

Serves 6
600 ml (1 pint) aspic jelly, made up according to packet instructions
225 g (8 oz) Stilton cheese, crumbled
1 tablespoon lemon juice
½ teaspoon white pepper
225 g (8 oz) cucumber, peeled and finely diced
300 ml (½ pint) double cream, lightly whipped
To garnish:
8–12 crisp, fresh lettuce leaves (optional)
1 whole cucumber, peeled and finely sliced
1 tablespoon finely chopped parsley

Preparation time: 15 minutes, plus chilling

1. Allow the aspic jelly to cool until it is just beginning to set. Place the cheese in a liquidizer or food processor. Add the aspic jelly, lemon juice and pepper and blend until the consistency of thin cream.
2. Pour the mixture into a mixing bowl and stir in the diced cucumber. Fold in the cream.
3. Rinse a 1.2 litre (2 pint) ring mould and pour in the mixture. Chill in the refrigerator for at least 2 hours, or overnight, until set.
4. To serve, turn the mousse out on to a serving plate lined with lettuce leaves. Arrange cucumber slices slightly overlapping round the sides and on top of the mousse and then sprinkle with parsley.
Variation: For a lunch or supper dish the centre of the ring can be filled with prawns or chopped chicken if liked.

PRAWNS IN ORANGES

⁓

This is an elegant first course from Sussex, ideal for a summer dinner party.

4 medium oranges
450 g (1 lb) peeled prawns, defrosted and drained if frozen
150 ml (¼ pint) cold white sauce, fairly thick (page 96)
150 ml (¼ pint) double cream
salt
white pepper
4 tablespoons crisp, finely shredded lettuce leaves
4 sprigs mint

Preparation time: 30 minutes, plus chilling
Cooking time: 10 minutes (for the sauce)

1. Carefully cut the tops off the oranges. Finely grate the rind from the orange tops. Scoop out all the pulp from the oranges, being careful not to break or pierce the shells. Pass the pulp through a sieve or juice extractor to extract the juice.
2. Mix the prawns into the white sauce and stir in the grated rind. Stir in the cream and 2 tablespoons of the orange juice.
3. Add salt and pepper to taste and spoon the mixture into the orange shells. Chill for 1 hour.
4. Serve the filled oranges on individual plates lined with shredded lettuce, each one garnished with a mint sprig.

CREAM OF SPINACH SOUP

One of the best vegetable soups, very quick and easy to make, as the spinach loses nothing of its flavour when frozen.

Serves 6
50 g (2 oz) butter
1 small onion, peeled and finely chopped
450 g (1 lb) frozen chopped spinach
900 ml (1½ pints) chicken stock
¼ teaspoon salt
¼ teaspoon freshly ground black pepper
2 teaspoons lemon juice
¼ teaspoon ground mace
15 g (½ oz) plain flour
4 tablespoons single cream

Preparation time: 5 minutes
Cooking time: 35 minutes

1. Melt half the butter in a large saucepan and gently fry the onion for about 5 minutes until soft but not brown. Add the spinach and stir from time to time until defrosted.
2. Add the stock, salt, pepper, lemon juice and mace. Bring to the boil, cover and simmer for about 15 minutes. Put the soup through a sieve or food processor and set it aside.
3. In a second saucepan, melt the remaining butter, sprinkle in the flour and cook, stirring, for 1 minute. Gradually pour in the spinach mixture, stirring constantly. Bring to the boil, then lower the heat and simmer gently for 5 minutes.
4. Taste and adjust the seasoning if necessary and just before serving, swirl in the cream.

From the left:
Cucumber and Stilton
mousse, Prawns in
oranges, Cream of
spinach soup

THREE WAYS OF COOKING SOLE

Dover soles are now so expensive that this wonderful fish is rarely served. However, since those caught off the South coast were considered best of all and those caught off Dover gave their name to the fish, it is a pity not to give two or three of the many ways of serving them. Lemon soles (sometimes called Witch soles) are much cheaper and can be cooked by exactly the same methods. They are very good indeed but not quite so firm in texture or so delicate in taste as the Dover sole.

1. GRILLED SOLE

8 fillets of sole or 4 small whole soles, skinned
1 tablespoon plain flour
salt
freshly ground black pepper
50–75 g (2–3 oz) butter, melted

Preparation time: 5 minutes
Cooking time: 6–8 minutes

1. Dust the fish on both sides with the flour. Season with salt and pepper. Brush the butter over the fish.
2. Grill under a preheated hot grill for about 3 minutes on each side for fillets, 4 minutes for whole fish. Pour more hot butter over the fish once or twice as it grills.

2. FRIED SOLE

1 tablespoon plain flour
salt
freshly ground black pepper
4 soles, skinned
1 egg, beaten
1 tablespoon milk
50 g (2 oz) fine dry breadcrumbs
vegetable oil for deep frying
To garnish:
lemon wedges
parsley sprigs

Preparation time: 5 minutes
Cooking time: 10 minutes

1. Season the flour with salt and pepper and use to dust the soles.
2. Put the beaten egg on a plate and stir in the milk. Spread out the breadcrumbs on a second plate. Dip the fish first in the egg, then in the breadcrumbs, pressing them on with the fingers, to coat thoroughly on both sides.
3. Heat the oil in a deep fryer to 180–190°C, 350–375°F, or until a cube of bread browns in 30 seconds. Deep fry the soles for 4–6 minutes, two at a time, until golden brown. Drain on kitchen paper and serve immediately, garnished with lemon wedges and parsley sprigs.

Variation: The soles can be shallow fried, for 3 minutes on each side, in half butter, half oil, if preferred.

3. POACHED SOLE

50 g (2 oz) butter
8 fillets of sole, halved
salt
freshly ground black pepper
300 ml (½ pint) dry white wine or milk
15 g (½ oz) plain flour
1 teaspoon lemon juice or ¼ teaspoon freshly grated nutmeg
1 tablespoon finely chopped parsley

Preparation time: 3 minutes
Cooking time: 30 minutes
Oven: 180°C, 350°F, Gas Mark 4

1. Butter an ovenproof dish. Use 25 g (1 oz) of the butter to spread each fillet with butter. Roll up as tightly as possible. Lay the rolled fillets side by side in the dish and season with salt and pepper.
2. Pour over the wine or milk, cover and bake in a preheated oven for 20 minutes.
3. Transfer the fish to a heated serving dish, cover and keep hot while making the sauce.
4. Melt the remaining butter, sprinkle in the flour and cook, stirring, for 1 minute. Gradually stir in the hot fish cooking liquid. Bring to the boil, then simmer for 2 minutes, stirring, and season to taste.
5. If wine was used, add a squeeze of lemon juice and 1 teaspoon of the parsley and stir well. If milk was used, replace the lemon juice with ¼ teaspoon nutmeg.
6. Pour the sauce over the fish, sprinkle with the remaining parsley and serve immediately with new potatoes and French beans.

From the top: Grilled sole, Fried sole, Poached sole

BEEF OLIVES

Serves 6
750 g (1½ lb) braising steak, cut very thin, or 6 flash
fry steaks, trimmed
forcemeat stuffing (page 20)
25 g (1 oz) plain flour
25 g (1 oz) butter or vegetable oil
1 medium onion, peeled and finely sliced
600 ml (1 pint) beef stock
150 ml (¼ pint) red wine
salt
freshly ground black pepper
1 tablespoon cornflour

Preparation time: 35 minutes
Cooking time: 1 hour 10 minutes
Oven: 180°C, 350°F, Gas Mark 4

1. Flatten the meat with a mallet or rolling pin
and cut it into 12 pieces, each about 7.5 × 10 cm
(3 × 4 inches).
2. Put a tablespoon of stuffing in the middle of
each slice and roll up neatly, tying each roll in two
places with thread.
3. Spread the flour out on a plate and roll each
olive in it, to coat thoroughly. Heat the butter or
oil in a frying pan and brown the olives quickly on
all sides. Transfer to a shallow ovenproof dish.
4. Add the onion to the fat in the frying pan and
fry gently for 3–4 minutes, then pour in the stock
and the wine. Bring to the boil and season to taste.
Pour evenly over the beef olives, cover and cook
in a preheated oven for 1 hour or until tender.
5. Carefully transfer the olives to a heated serving
plate and remove the thread. Keep hot.
6. Pour the cooking liquid into a saucepan and
bring to the boil. Mix the cornflour with a little
cold water, to make a smooth paste. Pour in a little
of the boiling stock and stir well, then pour back
into the stock in the saucepan, return to the boil
and boil gently for 2 minutes, stirring constantly.
7. Taste and adjust the seasoning, pour evenly
over the beef olives and serve immediately.

DEVILLED CHICKEN LEGS

2 teaspoons English mustard powder
1 teaspoon salt
½ teaspoon freshly ground black pepper
¼ teaspoon cayenne pepper
½ teaspoon paprika
2 teaspoons mild curry powder
3 teaspoons French mustard
50 g (2 oz) butter
8 cooked chicken legs
1 tablespoon plain flour
slices of hot buttered toast, to serve

Preparation time: 6 minutes
Cooking time: 6 minutes

1. Mix the mustard powder with half the salt,
pepper, cayenne and paprika, the curry powder
and French mustard and work to a paste. Add half
the butter and work until smooth.
2. Make 4 slits down the length of each chicken
leg and spread a little of the devil mixture into
each.
3. Season the flour with the remaining salt,
pepper, cayenne and paprika. Use to dust the
chicken legs. Melt the remaining butter and brush
over each leg.
4. Place under a preheated hot grill and grill the
joints for 6 minutes, turning to brown on all sides.
Baste with the pan juices once or twice.
5. Serve the chicken legs at once, on strips of hot
buttered toast.

From the bottom,
clockwise: *Devilled
chicken legs, Beef olives,
Tomato charlotte*

TOMATO CHARLOTTE

The basil and sugar bring out the flavour of the
tomatoes.

450 g (1 lb) tomatoes, skinned and sliced
2 teaspoons caster sugar
1 tablespoon chopped fresh basil or 1 teaspoon dried
basil
salt
freshly ground black pepper
100 g (4 oz) fresh white breadcrumbs
50 g (2 oz) butter

Preparation time: 15 minutes
Cooking time: 30 minutes
Oven: 180°C, 350°F, Gas Mark 4

1. Butter an ovenproof dish and put a layer of
tomato slices in it. Season with a little of the sugar,
basil, salt and pepper. Cover with a thin layer of
crumbs and dot with small pieces of butter.
2. Repeat these layers until all the ingredients are
used up, finishing with a layer of crumbs dotted
with butter.
3. Bake in a preheated oven for 30 minutes, or
until the top is brown and crisp.

SPATCH-COCKED POUSSINS

This recipe comes from Surrey.

4 poussins, about 225 g (8 oz) each
1 teaspoon salt
175 g (6 oz) butter, softened
4 streaky bacon rashers, rinded and halved
lengthways
Stuffing:
175 g (6 oz) fine fresh white breadcrumbs
75 g (3 oz) finely chopped mushrooms, lightly fried
2 teaspoons finely chopped parsley
2 egg yolks
salt
freshly ground black pepper
parsley sprigs, to garnish (optional)
Gravy:
15 g ($\frac{1}{2}$ oz) plain flour
300 ml ($\frac{1}{2}$ pint) chicken stock

Preparation time: 40 minutes
Cooking time: 30 minutes
Oven: 200°C, 400°F, Gas Mark 6

1. Mix all the ingredients for the stuffing thoroughly together. **A**
2. Using a very sharp, heavy knife, cut the poussins through the breast bone down to, but not through, the backbone. Open out, so that they lie flat, joined only by the backbone.
3. Rub with salt and spread with butter. Spoon a portion of stuffing on to each half poussin and flatten it, so that each half is filled and level.
4. Dot each bird with a little of the butter. Lay a bacon strip on each half poussin.
5. Butter a large baking sheet with 25 g (1 oz) of the butter and lay the poussins on it. Roast in the top part of a preheated oven for 10 minutes. Then very carefully turn and cook for a further 10 minutes. Turn back and cook for a further 2 minutes, to brown.
6. Transfer the poussins to a heated serving dish and keep hot while making the gravy. Heat the pan juices, sprinkle in the flour, scraping the base and sides of the tin with a wooden spoon, and cook, stirring, for 1–2 minutes. Gradually stir in the stock, bring to the boil and cook, stirring for 2–3 minutes. Taste and adjust the seasoning and hand separately in a heated gravy boat. Garnish the poussins with parsley sprigs, if liked.

A The stuffing can be prepared in the morning and kept in the refrigerator until required.

PORTMANTEAU LAMB CHOPS

Named because the opened chops, packed with liver and mushrooms, resemble the small travelling bag known as a portmanteau. Excellent for dinner with creamed potatoes.

4 loin chops, 4–5 cm (1$\frac{1}{2}$–2 inches) thick, trimmed
50 g (2 oz) butter, melted
8 chicken livers, trimmed and finely chopped
8 medium mushrooms, finely chopped
1 egg, beaten
50 g (2 oz) breadcrumbs
salt
freshly ground black pepper
To garnish:
grilled tomatoes
watercress sprigs

Preparation time: 15 minutes
Cooking time: 12 minutes
Oven: 200°C, 400°F, Gas Mark 6

1. Using a very sharp knife, slit the chops horizontally towards the bone, to make a pocket.
2. Heat half the butter in a frying pan, add the chicken livers and mushrooms and fry gently for 4–5 minutes, until soft but not browned. Cool slightly, then use to stuff the chops.
3. Sew up the stuffed chops with trussing thread. Dip each chop first in beaten egg, then in seasoned breadcrumbs, pressing them on with the fingers, to coat thoroughly. Place the chops in a baking dish, pour over the remaining melted butter and bake in a preheated oven for 7–10 minutes. Turn the chops and bake for a further 7–10 minutes. Serve immediately, garnished with grilled tomatoes and watercress sprigs.

SPRING VEGETABLES IN SAUCE

50 g (2 oz) butter
8 small young carrots, scraped
16 small new potatoes, scraped
16 spring onions, peeled and trimmed
bouquet of thyme, parsley and mint sprigs
1 tablespoon plain flour
300 ml ($\frac{1}{2}$ pint) chicken stock
150 ml ($\frac{1}{4}$ pint) dry white wine
225 g (8 oz) shelled peas, fresh or frozen
225 g (8 oz) shelled broad beans, fresh or frozen
1 teaspoon salt
1 teaspoon caster sugar
1 tablespoon double cream

Preparation time: 15 minutes
Cooking time: 20 minutes

1. Melt the butter in a saucepan, add the carrots, potatoes and spring onions and toss well to coat. Add the herbs.
2. Sprinkle in the flour. Gradually stir in the stock and wine. Cover and simmer for 10 minutes.

3. Stir in the peas and broad beans and simmer for a further 10 minutes until all the vegetables are tender.
4. Remove from the heat and stir in the salt, sugar and cream. Transfer to a heated serving dish and serve as a vegetarian main course garnished with croûtons or as an accompaniment to fish.

From the top: Portmanteau lamb chops, Spatch-cocked poussins, Spring vegetables in sauce

SALAMAGUNDY

Salamagundy, until recent years almost forgotten, was a famous dish in the eighteenth and nineteenth centuries. It is so ornamental that it was used as a centrepiece for a supper table on which other dishes were set out. It is always arranged on a large flat dish. In the centre is a small dish, standing on an inverted bowl, filled with an arrangement of parsley sprigs, herbs and some of the flowers or flower petals which used to be considered a delicacy: nasturtium flowers, with almost no stalk; a scattering of marigold petals; primrose or violet heads or a few rose petals.

In fact, it is a complete cold lunch or supper in itself, needing nothing but bread and butter to accompany it. This particular recipe comes from Hampshire. It is not a dish to make unless you have plenty of time and enjoy the idea of working slowly and carefully to make something not only delicious but ornamental.

Serves 6
150 ml (¼ pint) thick mayonnaise
1 iceberg lettuce, outer leaves discarded, very finely shredded
225 g (8 oz) boneless cooked chicken, skin removed and finely chopped
225 g (8 oz) cooked ham or tongue or a mixture of the two, cut into matchstick strips
1 cucumber, peeled and diced
2 tablespoons finely chopped parsley
6 hardboiled eggs, peeled and chopped
12 anchovy fillets, well drained, each cut into 4 pieces
225 g (8 oz) cooked beetroot, skinned and chopped
225 g (8 oz) celery stalks, chopped
225 g (8 oz) chicory, roughly chopped
225 g (8 oz) cooked peas, French beans or broad beans
225 g (8 oz) new potatoes, cooked and thinly sliced
1 small can sardines, drained and halved lengthways
12 shallots, or spring onions, peeled and finely chopped
8 tomatoes, skinned, seeded and chopped
12 small gherkins, sliced lengthways
12 parsley sprigs
To garnish:
nasturtium flowers, marigolds, rose petals, primroses, violets, etc. as available

Preparation time: at least 1 hour

1. Line a very large serving dish or tray with foil. In the centre invert a 1.25 litre (2 pint) pudding basin and put a small saucer or butter dish on top.
2. Spread the inverted bowl with the mayonnaise, using a pastry brush. Sprinkle it with shredded lettuce, pressing it on so that the sides of the bowl are completely covered.

3. Arrange a ring of chopped lettuce round the outer edge of the platter or tray. Within it, just touching, arrange a ring of chicken halfway round and ham or tongue or a mixture of the two, round the other half. Inside that arrange a ring of cucumber sprinkled with parsley, followed by a ring of chopped eggs with anchovies laid on them, a ring of beetroot, a ring of celery, chicory, peas, a ring of potatoes and sardines, until all the ingredients are used up. Mix the onions with the tomatoes to make the ring nearest the centre, around the bottom of the basin, and arrange the slices of gherkin up the sides of the bowl. Garnish with parsley sprigs wherever there are gaps. Arrange the flowers and flower petals in the saucer in the middle.
4. Serve with mayonnaise or vinaigrette dressing and crusty bread and butter.

BUTTERED HOP TOPS

This recipe from Kent can only be made with the very young top shoots of the hops, picked to only 4 leaves down the stem before or during May. Some people consider them more delicious than asparagus.

450 g (1 lb) hop shoots
50 g (2 oz) salt
50 g (2 oz) butter
¼ teaspoon freshly ground black pepper

Preparation time: 5 minutes, plus soaking
Cooking time: 10 minutes

1. Lay the shoots in a dish with enough cold water to cover and add the salt. Leave to soak for 2 hours.
2. Drain the hops and drop them into a saucepan containing enough boiling water to cover. Boil for 8 minutes.
3. Drain, chop coarsely and return to the pan. Stir in the butter and pepper and taste to see if more salt is required.
4. Stir for 30 seconds over gentle heat then serve in individual dishes as a starter, accompanied by brown bread and butter.

PORK WITH NUTS

This unusual roast comes from the New Forest. The pork was originally roasted over shelled beech nuts. Nowadays it is usually made with a mixture of chopped walnuts and almonds.

Serves 6
25 g (1 oz) plain flour
salt
freshly ground black pepper
1.75–2.25 kg (4–5 lb) top leg of pork
100g (4 oz) shelled walnuts, finely chopped
75 g (3 oz) blanched almonds, finely chopped
75 g (3 oz) fine fresh brown breadcrumbs
25 g (1 oz) butter
1.25 kg (2½ lb) potatoes, peeled and halved

Preparation time: 15 minutes
Cooking time: 2½ hours
Oven: 200°C, 400°F, Gas Mark 6

Left to right: *Pork with nuts, Spinach with cheese and eggs, Braised liver with nuts and raisins*

1. Season the flour with salt and pepper and rub all over the pork.
2. Mix the nuts with the breadcrumbs and ½ teaspoon salt. Butter a large roasting tin liberally and spoon the nut mixture down the centre. Work it with your hands to make a loose, flat cake.
3. Place a roasting rack over the nut mixture and set the pork on it. Roast in a preheated oven for 40 minutes.
4. Meanwhile, parboil the potatoes in salted water for 10 minutes. Remove the pork from the oven, baste well and put the potatoes in the tin, around the nut mixture. Return to the oven and roast for a further 1¾ hours, turning the potatoes and basting the pork from time to time.
5. When ready to serve, transfer the pork to a heated carving dish and the potatoes to a vegetable dish. Lift the nuts with a fish slice and sprinkle all over the joint. Serve with gravy and red-currant or crab-apple jelly.

SPINACH WITH CHEESE AND EGGS

This is a most delicious vegetarian dish for lunch or supper. The recipe comes from a manor house in Sussex.

Serves 6
1.5 kg (3 lb) fresh or frozen chopped spinach
90 g (3½ oz) butter
75 g (3 oz) plain flour
300 ml (½ pint) milk
175 g (6 oz) Cheddar cheese, grated
6 eggs, hardboiled and quartered

Preparation time: 30 minutes
Cooking time: 25 minutes

1. Cook the spinach in 2 tablespoons salted boiling water for 8 minutes or until just tender. Chop finely, then purée in a food processor.

2. Melt 75 g (3 oz) of the butter in a saucepan, sprinkle in the flour and cook, stirring for 1–2 minutes. Gradually stir in the milk, bring to the boil and cook, stirring, for 2–3 minutes, until thickened and smooth. Remove from the heat, add half the grated cheese and stir vigorously until melted.
3. Stir the spinach purée into the sauce, return to the heat and cook gently, stirring, until thoroughly heated through.
4. Pour the mixture into a large buttered ovenproof dish. Arrange the hardboiled egg quarters round the edge of the spinach mixture.
5. Sprinkle over the remaining grated cheese, dot with the remaining butter in small pieces and place under a preheated very hot grill until the cheese is bubbling and golden brown. Serve immediately.

BRAISED LIVER WITH NUTS AND RAISINS

This is an unusual and delicious way of serving braised liver. It comes from Marlow in Buckinghamshire.

50 g (2 oz) butter
2 medium onions, peeled and finely sliced
750 g (1½ lb) lambs' or calves' liver, cut into 1 cm
(½ inch) slices
25 g (1 oz) plain flour
50 g (2 oz) seedless raisins
1 teaspoon chopped fresh thyme or ½ teaspoon dried
thyme
150 ml (¼ pint) red wine
600 ml (1 pint) beef stock
salt
freshly ground black pepper
75 g (3 oz) blanched almonds, roughly chopped

Preparation time: 20 minutes
Cooking time: 1½ hours
Oven: 180°C, 350°F, Gas Mark 4

1. Melt half the butter in a frying pan, add the onions and fry for about 5 minutes, until soft.
2. Butter a fairly wide, shallow casserole. Dip the liver slices in the flour and lay half of them in the dish. Place the onions on top and sprinkle over half the raisins and the thyme. Top with the remaining liver and raisins.
3. Mix the wine with the stock, salt and pepper, and pour into the casserole. Cover closely with foil, then the lid, and cook for 1¼ hours.
4. Meanwhile, fry the almonds in the remaining butter until just golden brown.
5. Remove the liver from the oven, uncover and sprinkle the top with almonds. Return to the oven for 5 minutes before serving.

MACARONI PIE

Macaroni was first made and served in England in the Middle Ages and this type of pie, with its rich and varied filling, is also typical of the cooking of great houses at that period. It is an exciting and unexpected dish for a dinner or supper party and needs only a green salad as accompaniment.

Serves 8
600 ml (1 pint) well-seasoned white sauce (page 96)
150 ml ($\frac{1}{4}$ pint) double cream
450 g (1 lb) short-cut macaroni, cooked and drained
50 g (2 oz) butter
1 medium onion, peeled and finely sliced
225 g (8 oz) mushrooms, thinly sliced
750 g (1$\frac{1}{2}$ lb) boneless cooked chicken, skin removed and cut into 1 cm ($\frac{1}{2}$ inch) pieces
100 g (4 oz) cooked tongue, finely chopped
100 g (4 oz) lean cooked ham, finely chopped
75 g (3 oz) Cheddar cheese, grated
225 g (8 oz) peeled prawns, defrosted and drained if frozen
25 g (1 oz) Parmesan cheese, grated
16 triangles of flaky pastry (page 61) baked to a light golden brown

Preparation time: 45 minutes
Cooking time: 1 hour 20 minutes
Oven: 180°C, 350°F, Gas Mark 4

1. Heat the white sauce to just below boiling point. Stir in the cream, remove from the heat and cool slightly, then stir in the cooked macaroni.
2. Heat half the butter in a frying pan. Add the onion and fry for about 5 minutes until soft, then add the mushrooms and fry gently for a further 5 minutes.
3. Arrange half the chicken in the base of a large, greased ovenproof dish, about 10 cm (4 inches) deep and sprinkle half the tongue, ham and mushroom mixture on top. Scatter with half the Cheddar cheese and spoon over a 2.5 cm (1 inch) layer of the macaroni in sauce. Scatter over the prawns and spoon another layer of macaroni on top. Make layers of chicken, tongue, ham and mushroom mixture and finally top with the remaining macaroni in sauce. Sprinkle with the remaining Cheddar cheese.
4. Stand the dish in a roasting tin and pour in boiling water to come halfway up the sides of the dish. Bake in a preheated oven for 50 minutes.
5. Remove from the oven and sprinkle the top with the Parmesan cheese. Dot with the remaining butter. Return to the oven for a further 10 minutes. Place the pastry triangles on a baking sheet and heat through in the lower part of the oven.
6. Serve the macaroni pie with the hot pastry triangles.

OAST CAKES

Oasts are the brick buildings in which hops are dried. These cakes were made by the Kentish hop pickers to eat in the hop gardens. The dough was mixed early in the day and set aside. It was made into small balls and fried over the camp fire at the afternoon break. The hop pickers shallow-fried them in lard, but they are much better deep-fried.

Serves 6
450 g (1 lb) plain flour
½ teaspoon salt
100 g (4 oz) lard, diced
100 g (4 oz) currants
4 tablespoons beer or ale
4 tablespoons water
vegetable oil for deep frying
50 g (2 oz) caster sugar

Preparation time: 5 minutes
Cooking time: 8–10 minutes

1. Sift the flour with the salt into a mixing bowl. Add the lard and rub in with the fingertips until the mixture resembles fine breadcrumbs.
2. Stir in the currants and mix to a stiff dough with the beer and 4 tablespoons of water.
3. Heat the vegetable oil in a deep fryer to 180°–190°C, 350°–375°F, or until a bread cube browns in 30 seconds.
4. Shape the dough into balls and deep-fry, a few at a time, until golden brown all over. Drain quickly on kitchen paper, roll in caster sugar and serve immediately.

From the left:
Triangles of flaky pastry, Macaroni pie, Oast cakes

KENTISH PUDDING PIE

This very good pudding was hardly known outside Kent until recent times. Even today, if it is served in another part of England, the cook almost always turns out to be Kentish.

Serves 4–6
900 ml (1½ pints) milk
100 g (4 oz) ground rice
225 g (8 oz) shortcrust pastry
120 g (4½ oz) butter
50 g (2 oz) caster sugar
3 eggs
50 g (2 oz) sultanas, raisins or currants
¼ teaspoon freshly grated nutmeg
2 tablespoons double cream

Preparation time: 30 minutes
Cooking time: 45 minutes
Oven: 180°C, 350°F, Gas Mark 4

1. Pour the milk into a saucepan and stir in the ground rice. Bring to the boil, then lower the heat and cook, stirring, for 10 minutes or until the mixture thickens. Remove from the heat and allow to cool for 15 minutes.
2. Meanwhile, line a pie dish with the pastry, turning the crust over the edge of the dish and marking it with a fork.
3. Cream 100 g (4 oz) of the butter with the sugar until light, fluffy and pale, then beat in the eggs. Stir the mixture into the ground rice and milk, add the dried fruit and nutmeg and beat well. Stir in the cream.
4. Pour the mixture into the pie dish and dot with the remaining butter. Bake in the centre of a preheated oven for 35 minutes. Serve hot or cold.

SUSSEX POND PUDDING

This is the best of all suet puddings. When the crust is cut the melted butter and sugar flow out and form a pond on the dish around the pudding.

Serves 6
15 g (½ oz) butter, softened
350 g (12 oz) suet crust (page 122)
100 g (4 oz) unsalted butter, well chilled
175 g (6 oz) demerara sugar
1 large lemon

Preparation time: 20 minutes
Cooking time: 3¼ hours

1. Grease a 900 ml (1½ pint) pudding basin with the butter. Roll out the suet crust about 2.5 cm (1 inch) thick. Reserve one quarter for the lid and use the large piece to line the basin.
2. Cut the chilled butter into 8 pieces and put 4 of them into the lined basin, together with half the sugar.
3. Prick the lemon all over with a sharp skewer or knife and press one end into the butter and sugar mixture, so that it stands upright. Press the remaining butter and sugar around and over the lemon.
4. Dampen the edge of the crust at the top of the basin. Roll out the reserved suet crust to a circle for the lid and use to cover the basin, pressing the edges together firmly, to seal. Cover closely with foil and place a saucer over the foil.
5. Pour about 7.5 cm (3 inches) of water into a large saucepan and bring to the boil. Stand the pudding in the saucepan and cover with the lid. Boil gently for 3 hours, topping up with more boiling water as necessary.
6. Lift the basin from the saucepan, remove the foil and invert on to a large serving plate to unmould. If liked, put the pudding in a very low oven to dry off for a few minutes. Cut into wedges at the table, so that the 'pond' of sugar and butter can be seen as it runs out. Spoon some over each serving. Cut the lemon into slices and serve a slice with each portion.

CHERRIES HOT

This is an early recipe from the famous cherry orchards of Kent. If using canned, sweetened cherries, omit the sugar when cooking them.

1 egg
300 ml (½ pint) milk
50 g (2 oz) caster sugar
4 large slices white bread, each about 5 mm (¼ inch) thick, crusts removed
350 g (12 oz) ripe fresh cherries, stoned
40 g (1½ oz) butter
whipped cream, to serve

Preparation time: 15 minutes
Cooking time: 10 minutes

1. Beat the egg with the milk and 15 g (½ oz) of the sugar. Cut the slices of bread in half and soak in the egg mixture for 5 minutes, turning to make sure they soak evenly.
2. Place the cherries in a small saucepan with 25 g (1 oz) of the sugar and heat slowly until almost boiling. Leave the pan over the lowest heat so that the cherries remain hot but do not continue to cook.
3. Heat the butter in a large frying pan until just foaming. Put in the bread and fry on both sides until it is golden brown, crisp on the outside and

soft inside.

4. Place 4 pieces of the bread on a warmed dish and, using a perforated spoon, lift a quarter of the cherries on to each. Place the remaining pieces of bread on top and sprinkle each sandwich with the remaining sugar. Hand the hot cherry juice separately as a sauce. Serve with whipped cream.

From the top: *Kentish pudding pie, Sussex pond pudding, Cherries hot*

NORTHERN IRELAND

For a long time, Northern Ireland has been known for the purity and excellent quality of its food. In the main, the cooking is simple, and makes good use of the fine natural flavours of the foods. Basically, it is a country kitchen cuisine, and the smell of brown bread baking, bacon cooking and big pots bubbling on the stove come to mind whenever Irish food is thought of, or talked about.

There are the grand dishes, the sides of smoked salmon and the luscious steaks, but there is also the simpler traditional food which uses local ingredients at their best. You will not find elaborate methods used in this cooking but good butter, cream, and, of course, the native drinks such as Guinness or Irish whiskey. The potato of course appears in many forms, from the potato cake, called fadge, served for breakfast with bacon and eggs, to the world-famous Irish Stew which is rich and creamy when made properly.

However, it is in baking that the Ulster housewife excels, with many varieties of breads and cakes such as soda bread, Barm Brack, spice bread and whiskey cake. Such items were for some time frowned on as they were considered too fattening but nowadays with the recognised need for an increase of fibre in the diet, they are coming back into their own. Soda bread is traditionally served with another speciality: herrings baked in Guinness – food for the gods.

Cushendall Bay, Co Antrim

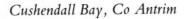

BACON BROTH

This is not a broth in the ordinary sense of the word but more like a Scotch broth or the French *pot-au-feu*, in that the soup was often drunk first, then the meat served as a second course with vegetables. Other meats or game, such as mutton, beef or rabbit, can also be used either in place of the bacon or with it.

Serves 4–6

900 g (2 lb) shoulder or collar bacon, soaked overnight
2 tablespoons pearl barley
2 tablespoons red lentils
2 medium onions, peeled and sliced
4–6 medium carrots, scraped and sliced
2 medium parsnips, peeled and sliced
freshly ground black pepper
1 sprig thyme
1 sprig parsley
450 g (1 lb) potatoes, peeled and sliced
1 small cabbage, quartered
1 leek, chopped
1 tablespoon chopped parsley

Preparation time: 30 minutes, plus soaking overnight
Cooking time: 1–1¼ hours

1. Strain the soaked bacon and scrape the skin, then put into a large saucepan with water to cover. Bring to the boil and remove any scum from the top.
2. Add the pearl barley and the lentils, bring to the boil and simmer for about 25 minutes.
3. Add the onions, carrots, parsnips, pepper to taste, thyme and parsley sprig. Bring back to the boil, lower heat, cover and simmer gently for half an hour.
4. Add the potatoes and the cabbage, bring back to the boil again and simmer until they are tender but not mushy. The barley and lentils will be soft by this time, and the piece of bacon should be cooked through. If not, simmer a little longer.
5. Five minutes before the broth is ready, add the chopped leek and the chopped parsley.
6. To serve, lift out the bacon and skin it. Then either chop it into chunks or, if serving the soup first, keep it as a joint and carve.

HERRINGS POTTED IN GUINNESS

These herrings are delicious served with buttered brown soda bread. They will keep refrigerated for 1 week.

4 fresh herrings, filleted
2 bay leaves
1 onion, peeled and sliced
4 whole cloves
6 black peppercorns
6 white peppercorns
150 ml (¼ pint) Guinness or stout
150 ml (¼ pint) malt vinegar
1 teaspoon sea salt

Preparation time: 30 minutes
Cooking time: 40 minutes
Oven: 180°C, 350°F, Gas Mark 4

1. Roll up the herring fillets with a piece of bay leaf inside each and arrange in an ovenproof dish.
2. Arrange the onion rings over and scatter the cloves and peppercorns around.
3. Carefully pour over the Guinness or stout and vinegar.
4. Scatter over the sea salt, cover with foil and bake in the centre of the preheated oven for 40 minutes.
5. Cool in the liquid and serve cold.

COD'S ROE FRITTERS

Cod's roe is a seasonal delicacy from February to March. It is often served as a breakfast dish in Ireland with fried or grilled bacon rashers.

Serves 4–6

450 g (1 lb) fresh cod's roe, cooked and peeled
2 rounded tablespoons plain flour
1 egg (size 1), beaten
2–3 tablespoons bacon fat or oil
wedges of lemon
French toast:
1 egg (size 1)
3 tablespoons milk
4–6 large slices white crustless bread

Preparation time: 30 minutes
Cooking time: 15 minutes

1. Cut the cod's roe into slices about 1 cm (½ inch) thick and roll in the flour.
2. Dip the floured roe slices in the egg, then roll in the flour again and set aside.
3. Make the French toast by beating the egg with the milk and dipping the bread slices into it on both sides. They should be well covered.
4. Heat the bacon fat or oil and quickly fry the soaked bread in it, turning once, until a pale gold. Keep warm.
5. In the same oil or fat, adding a little more if necessary, fry the cod's roe fritters on both sides until golden. Arrange on the French toast and put a wedge of lemon on each plate.

From the top, clockwise: Bacon broth, Herrings potted in Guinness, Cod's roe fritters, Brown soda bread (page 152)

BAKED ULSTER HAM

Irish hams are world famous for their sweetness and succulence.

Serves 8

1.75 kg (4 lb) corner of gammon, soaked overnight
2 whole cloves
4 black peppercorns
1 teaspoon brown sugar
Topping:
25 g (1 oz) butter
50 g (2 oz) brown sugar
pinch of ground cinnamon
1 tablespoon Bushmill's whiskey
150 ml ($\frac{1}{4}$ pint) Guinness

Preparation time: 20 minutes, plus soaking overnight
Cooking time: 2 hours
Oven: 190°C, 375°F, Gas Mark 5

1. Strain the soaked gammon and scrape the outer skin, then put into a large saucepan and barely cover with cold water, adding the cloves, peppercorns and sugar.
2. Bring to the boil, remove any scum, then reduce to a simmer. Cover and cook for $1\frac{1}{2}$ hours.
3. Remove the gammon, cool slightly but do not let it get cold, and peel off the skin.
4. To make the topping, mix the butter, brown sugar, cinnamon and whiskey together well. Score the top of the gammon fat with a diamond pattern and press the topping on to it firmly.
5. Lift on to an ovenproof dish and pour the Guinness or stout around.
6. Bake in the preheated oven for about 30 minutes or until the topping is crisp and golden. Serve hot or cold.

IRISH STEW

One of the oldest Irish recipes in existence and known all over the world. It is frequently spoilt by the use of too much liquid and by the addition of other vegetables. It should be creamy and fresh tasting.

1.5–1.75 kg (3¼–4 lb) lean neck of lamb, boned and trimmed
450 g (1 lb) onions, peeled and sliced
900 g (2 lb) potatoes, peeled and sliced
salt
freshly ground black pepper
1 tablespoon chopped parsley
pinch of dried thyme
600 ml (1 pint) beef stock

Preparation time: 35 minutes
Cooking time: 2 hours
Oven: 160°C, 325°F, Gas Mark 3

1. Cut the meat into fairly large pieces.
2. Layer the meat in an ovenproof dish with the onions and potatoes, seasoning each layer very well, adding the parsley and thyme. End with a layer of potatoes.
3. Pour in the stock, cover with a piece of buttered foil and a tight–fitting lid and cook in the preheated oven for about 2 hours.
4. If the stew looks dry towards the end of the cooking time, add a little extra stock.

STUFFED PORK STEAK

Serves 6
2 pork fillets, weighing about 1.4 kg (3 lb), trimmed
175 g (6 oz) fresh breadcrumbs
3 tablespoons milk
1 medium onion, peeled and finely chopped
1 teaspoon grated lemon rind
1 teaspoon lemon juice
pinch of ground nutmeg or mace
½ teaspoon dried sage
½ teaspoon dried thyme
1 tablespoon chopped parsley
salt
freshly ground black pepper
50 g (2 oz) butter
300 ml (½ pint) beef stock

Preparation time: 40 minutes
Cooking time: 1½ hours
Oven: 200°C, 400°F, Gas Mark 6
then: 180°C, 350°F, Gas Mark 4

1. Lay the pork fillets on a board and cut down the middle, not right through the meat, so you can pull the 2 sides apart. Gently spread them open and beat down with the blunt side of the knife so that they are almost flat. Score them lightly down the length, again not cutting right through, so that they have a flattish rectangular shape.
2. Make the stuffing by mixing together the breadcrumbs, milk, onion, lemon rind and juice, spice, herbs, salt and pepper, to form a thick paste.
3. Divide the stuffing between the 2 pork steaks and either fold them over sideways or roll up, in either case securing with a cocktail stick.
4. Rub all over with the butter, season lightly and put into a roasting pan.
5. Add the stock, cover loosely with foil and put into the preheated oven for 20 minutes, then reduce the temperature and cook for 1 hour.
6. Baste once or twice and turn each pork steak if necessary. Take off the foil 10 minutes from the end and brown the tops a little.
7. To make the gravy, transfer the meat to a serving dish and keep warm. Put the roasting pan on the stove and scrape down the sides, boil up the liquid to reduce a little, then add seasoning.

From the top, clockwise: *Irish stew, Stuffed pork steak, Baked Ulster ham*

BROWN SODA BREAD

The most traditional food in Ireland, still made weekly in countless homes.

225 g (8 oz) wholemeal flour
225 g (8 oz) plain white flour
1 teaspoon baking soda
3 teaspoons baking powder
2 teaspoons salt
450 ml (¾ pint) buttermilk or sour milk or 300 ml
(½ pint) natural unsweetened yoghurt and 150 ml
(¼ pint) water, mixed
1 egg, beaten

Preparation time: 15 minutes
Cooking time: 45–50 minutes
Oven: 190°C, 375°F, Gas Mark 5

1. Sift together the flours, baking soda, baking powder and salt.
2. Mix the buttermilk and beaten egg and stir in.
3. Knead on a floured surface for a few minutes until smooth, then shape by hand either into a round flat cake, or put into a 900 g (2 lb) greased loaf tin.
4. Make a deep cross on the round or cut down the middle of the tin to ensure even distribution in rising, and bake in the preheated oven for about 40–45 minutes.
5. If a glaze is required, take out and brush with a little warm milk or beaten egg and put back in the oven for about 5 minutes.
6. Wrap in a tea towel to keep the crust soft and cool before cutting. F
7. If preferred the mixture can be shaped into small scones and baked for 15 minutes.
F When completely cold these loaves will freeze very well sealed in a plastic bag. Thaw out for at least 3 hours before cutting.

SPICE BREAD

This bread will keep moist for some days wrapped in a cloth and almost improves with keeping.

Makes one 1 kg (2 lb) loaf
275 g (10 oz) self-raising flour, sifted
1 teaspoon mixed spice
½ teaspoon ground ginger
100 g (4 oz) light brown sugar
25 g (1 oz) candied peel, chopped
175 g (6 oz) sultanas
50 g (2 oz) butter
100 g (4 oz) golden syrup
1 egg (size 1) beaten
4 tablespoons milk

Preparation time: 30 minutes
Cooking time: 1¼ hours
Oven: 180°C, 350°F, Gas Mark 4; then 160°C, 325°F, Gas Mark 3

1. Sift the flour with the spice and ginger, then add the brown sugar, candied peel and sultanas. Make a well in the centre.
2. Melt the butter with the golden syrup over a low heat, but do not allow it to become too hot.
3. Pour into the well in the mixture and mix thoroughly.
4. Mix the beaten egg with the milk and add to the flour, mixing very well.
5. Grease a 1 kg (2 lb) loaf tin and pour the mixture in, levelling off the top.
6. Bake in the preheated oven for 30 minutes, then lower the heat and cook for another 45 minutes. Test with a thin skewer before taking out. The skewer should come out clean if the loaf is cooked.
7. Turn out on to a wire tray to cool.

BARM BRACK

There is a yeasted version of barm brack which is traditionally eaten at Hallowe'en, but this recipe is made more frequently. 'Brack' comes from the Irish word *breac* which means speckled, in this case with the fruit.

Makes 3 cakes
450 g (1 lb) sultanas
450 g (1 lb) raisins
450 g (1 lb) brown sugar
3 cups of milkless tea
450 g (1 lb) plain flour
3 eggs, beaten
3 teaspoons baking powder
3 teaspoons mixed spice
1 tablespoon honey, warmed

Preparation time: 30 minutes, plus soaking overnight
Cooking time: 1½ hours
Oven: 160°C, 325°F, Gas Mark 3

1. Soak the fruit and sugar in the tea overnight.
2. The next day add the rest of the ingredients except the honey and mix very well.
3. Lightly grease three 20 cm (8 inch) round tins and divide the mixture between them, levelling off the tops.
4. Bake in the preheated oven for 1½ hours, then take out and brush the tops with a little warmed honey to glaze.
5. Put back in the oven for 5 minutes to dry.
6. Cool on a wire tray.

IRISH WHISKEY CAKE

Makes 1 × 17.5 cm (7 inch) cake
peel of 1 large lemon
85 ml (3 fl oz) Irish whiskey
175 g (6 oz) butter
175 g (6 oz) caster sugar
3 eggs, separated
175 g (6 oz) plain flour, sifted
175 g (6 oz) sultanas
pinch of salt
1 teaspoon baking powder

Preparation time: 30 minutes plus soaking
overnight
Cooking time: 1½–1¾ hours
Oven: 180°C, 350°F, Gas Mark 4

1. Put the lemon peel into a glass, cover with the whiskey and leave overnight, covered.
2. Cream the butter and sugar until light.
3. Add the egg yolks one at a time with a spoonful of sifted flour, mixing well.
4. Strain the whiskey into it and add the sultanas with 2 tablespoons flour.
5. Whisk the egg whites stiffly and fold into the mixture with the remaining flour mixed with the salt and baking powder. See that the mixture is well amalgamated.
6. Pour into a greased and lined 17.5 cm (7 inch) cake tin and bake in the preheated oven for 1½–1¾ hours. Test with a skewer before taking from the oven – the skewer should come out clean.
7. Cool for 5 minutes in the tin, then turn out on to a wire tray and remove the paper.

From the top: *Barm brack, Irish whiskey cake, Spice bread*

BLACKCAP PUDDING

This pudding was originally made with black raspberries, a very dark red raspberry hardly ever grown these days except in long-established kitchen gardens.

Serves 4–6
½ *tablespoon butter*
175 g (6 oz) *blackcurrants, topped and tailed*
½ *teaspoon lemon juice*
2 *heaped tablespoons sugar*
75 g (3 oz) *self-raising flour, sifted*
150 g (5 oz) *fresh breadcrumbs*
2 *eggs (size 1), beaten*
300 ml (½ pint) *milk*

Preparation time: 30 minutes
Cooking time: 2½ hours

1. Butter a 1 litre (2 pint) pudding basin.
2. Put the blackcurrants in a saucepan with the lemon juice and half the sugar and cook gently for about 5 minutes. Transfer to the basin.
3. Put the flour into a bowl, add the breadcrumbs and remaining sugar and mix well.
4. Make a well in the middle, add the beaten eggs and mix again. Finally add the milk and stir it in thoroughly.
5. Leave to stand for about 15 minutes.
6. Pour the mixture over the blackcurrants, cover with a piece of buttered paper or foil and tie down firmly.
7. Steam over boiling water for 2–2½ hours.
8. Turn out on to a warmed plate or dish, reversing the basin so that the 'black cap' covers the pudding and runs down the sides. Serve with double or whipping cream.

IRISH COFFEE

Serves 1
sugar to taste
150 ml (¼ pint) *strong, black coffee, hot*
45 ml (1½ fl oz) *Irish whiskey*
1 *tablespoon thick double or whipping cream*

Preparation time: 5 minutes

1. Warm a stemmed goblet glass and put in the sugar, to taste.
2. Add the hot coffee to within 3 cm (1½ inches) of the top, stir well and quickly to dissolve the sugar.
3. Add the Irish whiskey to fill up to 1 cm (½ inch) below the rim.
4. Hold a teaspoon with its curved side upper-most across the top of the glass tilting a little downwards to the hot liquid. Dribble the cream over the teaspoon so that it settles on the top of the coffee but does not sink into it.
5. Do not stir, but drink the whiskey-coffee through the cream.

CARRAGEEN PUDDING WITH HONEY AND LEMON

Carrageen is a branching seaweed found all around the coast of Ireland. It is dried and used extensively for puddings and also for a syrup to ease sore throats. It has great gelatinous properties and is full of minerals. There is no taste of the sea when it is used properly. Many health food shops sell it, already dried and prepared for use.

Serves 4–6
40 g (1½ oz) *carrageen moss*
2 *heaped teaspoons honey*
1 *tablespoon lemon juice*
finely grated lemon rind, to decorate
150 ml (¼ pint) *double or whipping cream, whipped*
1 *egg white, stiffly beaten*
finely grated rind of 1 lemon

Preparation time: 1 hour
Cooking time: 30 minutes

1. Soak the carrageen in hot water to cover for about 15 minutes, then drain well, discarding the liquid.
2. Put the carrageen into 600 ml (1 pint) cold fresh water with the honey, lemon juice and grated rind. Bring to the boil and simmer for 25–30 minutes.
3. Strain, discarding the carrageen, and let the liquid cool.
4. When the liquid is cold and the consistency of a raw egg, gently fold in first the cream, then the stiffly beaten egg white.
5. Rinse out a mould with cold water. Without drying it first, pour in the mixture, then chill until set. Alternatively it can be poured into individual glasses or dishes. Decorate with finely grated lemon rind.

*From the bottom,
Clockwise: Carrageen pudding with honey and lemon, Irish coffee, Blackcap pudding*

INDEX

ACKNOWLEDGEMENTS

Special photography by Laurie Evans with stylist Leslie Richardson
Food prepared for photography by Liz and Pete, Jane Suthering and Michelle Thomson

Other photography: James Davis Photo Library 7 top, 50–1, 100–1; Robert Estall 64–5;
Spectrum Colour Library 8, 9, 30–1, 128–9; Tony Stone Associates 82–3;
ZEFA Picture Library 7 below, 10–11, 118–9, 146–7

Front cover illustration by Sue Lines
Back cover photography: Left: Laurie Evans; Above right: ZEFA Picture Library;
Below right: Tony Stone Associates